WOMEN IN SOCIETY

ISRAEL
BETH UVAL

MARSHALL CAVENDISH
New York • London • Sydney

Reference edition published 1993 by
Marshall Cavendish Corporation
2415 Jerusalem Avenue
P.O. Box 587
North Bellmore
New York 11710

© Times Editions Pte Ltd 1993

Originated and designed by
Times Books International, an imprint of
Times Editions Pte Ltd

All rights reserved. No part of this book may be reproduced or utilized in any form or by any means electronic or mechanical, including photocopying, recording, or by an information storage and retrieval system, without permission from the copyright holder.

Printed in Singapore

Cover picture by Mike Evans/Life File

Library of Congress Cataloging-in-Publication Data:
Uval, Beth.
    Women in society. Israel / Beth Uval.
      p. cm. — (Women in society)
    Includes bibliographical references and index.
    Summary: Examines the experiences of women in Israel society, discussing their participation in various fields and profiling the lives of significant women.
    ISBN 1–85435–503–1 :
    1. Women—Israel—Social conditions—Juvenile literature.
    [1. Women—Israel. 2. Israel—Social conditions.]
    I. Title.
    II. Series: Women in society (New York, N.Y.)
HQ1728.5.U93 1992
305.42' 095694—dc20   92–12372
                                  CIP
                                   AC

Women in Society

Editorial Director	Shirley Hew
Managing Editor	Shova Loh
Editors	Goh Sui Noi
	Roseline Lum
	June Khoo Ai Lin
	Debra Fernando
	MaryLee Knowlton
	Junia Baker
	Sue Sismondo
Picture Editor	Nancy Yong
Production	Edmund Lam
Design	Tuck Loong
	Ong Su Ping
	Ang Siew Lian
Illustrations	Eric Siow/AC Graphic

25.95

Introduction

Israel is a young country with a long history. Established as a modern state on May 14, 1948, Israel is deeply rooted in thousands of years of tradition. The lives of Israeli women are shaped by both the urgent demands of a rapidly developing young country and the equally compelling power of centuries of custom. Each woman responds differently to these forces. There is thus no typical Israeli woman, but rather a complex and constantly changing mosaic of individuals, each shaped by her national, religious, and ethnic origins; her relation to the traditions she has inherited; her political attitudes; her own unique personality.

Coming from over 50 countries around the world, Israelis represent a rainbow of cultures, each with its own models of how women should live their lives. Rubbing shoulders on the same Jerusalem street are women from Kiev, Addis Ababa, Baghdad, New York, and maybe a village near Bethlehem. Each faces her own dilemmas of tradition and change, her own hard choices and decisions. Traditions exert a powerful hold; new possibilities open daily. There are no easy answers.

Ever-present for each is the complex political and military conflict that touches every aspect of women's lives, among both the Jewish majority and the Arab communities that constitute 18 % of Israel's population. In these pages, you will meet some of the women who make up the Israeli mosaic and see how they deal with the special challenges they face.

Contents

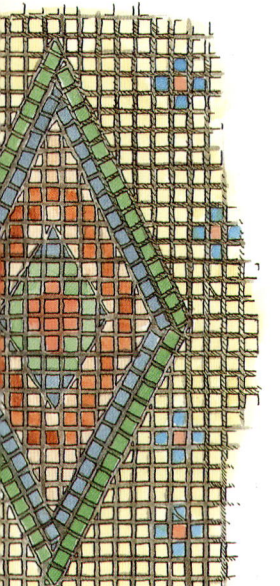

Bruria 7
A scholar and gentlewoman • Bruria's daughters

Milestones 11
Biblical women • Women in Jewish law • Women in early Christianity • Women in Islam • The Jewish return • The pioneers • Women farmers • The women's agricultural training farm • The kibbutz • Building • Getting the vote • Arms and the woman: defense • 1948: The state of Israel is born • Mass immigration • Inequality and advancement • In the Arab community • Women and the law • The kibbutz today

Women in Society 37
Education • Social work • Immigrant absorption • Hebrew language teaching • Medicine • Law • Politics • Theater • Sports • Literature

Being Woman 59
Immigration • The Yemenites • The Ethiopians • Traditions and transitions • Jewish religious life • Ultra-Orthodox women • Arab women • Druze women • Christian women • War and peace • Women in the military

Profiles of Women 81
Hannah Senesh • Golda Meir • Shoshana Damari • Ida Nudel • Maryam Mar'i • Leah Shakdiel

A Lifetime 103
Birth • School • High school • Youth movements • Coming of age • Army service • Dating • Marriage • The wedding ceremony • Home and family • Pro-children policies • Sharing roles • The calendar • Jewish calendar • Grandmothers

Women Firsts 124

Glossary 126

Bibliography 127

Index 128

chapter one

Bruria

The Bruria tales are the saga of an exceptional woman, a leading scholar and legal authority at a time when learning belonged almost exclusively to men.

The Bruria stories developed over hundreds of years, with various accounts recorded between the 2nd and 11th centuries. Part fact and part legend, the Bruria tales illustrate not precise historical truth, but rather the truth of attitudes—how the people who passed on the stories from generation to generation, century after century, felt about women. And what they felt, as the tales show, is complex and at times contradictory.

A scholar and gentlewoman

Bruria was probably born in the first quarter of the 2nd century and lived in Tiberias, in what is now northern Israel. The daughter of a great scholar and the wife of a renowned sage, Rabbi Meir, Bruria was unusually educated for a woman of her time. The first stories of Bruria, as recorded in the Talmud (the compendium of Jewish religious law and tradition), are all positive and admiring. She excelled in her knowledge of the Jewish religious and legal tradition, an achievement that held the highest status in her society. She was held up as an example to men. In one tale, a student proposed to learn a certain difficult book within three months. His teacher ridiculed him, saying that even Bruria, "who studied 300 laws from 300 teachers in a day," could not finish learning the book in three years.

Opposite: Water Carriers, a painting by Moshe Castel.

Right: A woman dressed in the clothes of Bruria's time.

The Precious Trust

In what is perhaps the most famous tale, the two sons of Bruria and Meir die on the Sabbath. In order not to disturb the sanctity of the day, Bruria avoids breaking the terrible news to her husband until the Sabbath is ended. In the evening, she says to him, "Some time ago, someone came and left something valuable in my trust. Now he has come to take it back. Shall I return it to him or not?" Meir naturally tells her to return the property to its owner. Bruria then leads him into the room where their two dead sons are. When Meir begins to weep, Bruria says, "Did you not tell me that we must return what was given in trust? The Lord has given, and the Lord has taken away. Blessed be the name of the Lord."

Bruria is the only woman in Talmudic literature whose views were taken seriously by the scholars of her time. Her opinions were respected and laws were based on them.

Bruria also held the extraordinary position of teaching men. In one anecdote, she rebukes a student for learning in an undertone and urges him to study out loud, so that his learning be "ordered and sure."

Other tales illustrate Bruria's moral virtues.

In one story, Bruria's husband, Rabbi Meir, prays for the death of certain bandits who are plaguing the neighborhood. Bruria reminds him of a verse in the Book of Psalms that says "Let sins end." Interpreting the verse to mean sins and not sinners, she urges Meir to pray for the bandits' repentance rather than for their death. He does as she says, and the criminals mend their ways.

Paradoxically, the tradition in which Bruria was such an expert did not encourage and, according to some, did not allow women to become scholars of the tradition. The sages debated whether women were permitted to study at all. Some held that a father was obligated to teach his daughters just as he was obligated to teach his sons. Others declared that there was no point in teaching women, for they were light-minded, foolish, and incompetent. In some of the Bruria tales, she ironically mocks these disparaging views of women.

It was one such incident, according to a legend first recorded in the 11th century, that brought about Bruria's tragic end. When Bruria ridicules the saying that women are light-minded, her husband warns her that her own fate could yet prove the truth of these words. He then persuades one of his young students to try to seduce her. When, after many days, she feels herself yielding to the student's advances, Bruria strangles herself, and Rabbi Meir flees from the land in shame and disgrace. This tale contrasts strangely with the other stories of the virtuous Bruria and Meir, and its inclusion in the tradition says much about the mixed attitude toward women who excelled in what was usually a man's sphere. On the one hand, Bruria was respected for her learning, her righteousness, and her piety. On the other, her womanhood was used to bring about her downfall.

Bruria's daughters

The passage of hundreds of years has not made the tale of Bruria any less disturbing, for the contradictory attitudes toward women that the tale shows are still with us. Women who create new roles, especially in what have traditionally been the male areas of religious life, are respected and admired by some, and viewed with discomfort and suspicion by others. Today's pioneering women rabbis—Bruria's spiritual daughters—are just one example.

The dilemma of Bruria—of the woman who takes on roles that are exceptional for her time—has yet to be resolved. There has always been a tension between women's biological functions as wife and mother and women's other pursuits. Israel now has many models of women who are active in society, and laws stating equal rights for men and women. But what the Bruria stories illustrate is attitude—and attitudes change less easily than laws.

Were Bruria alive today, she would still be exceptional for her learning and righteousness—but she would not be alone. During recent years, a growing number of Israeli women have been studying the sources of their tradition and creating new roles for women within it. Forging new combinations between old and new, family and work, home and community, these women are writing a new chapter of the Bruria story. Taking up the challenge of creating a world in which Bruria would thrive, they are giving her tale a happier ending.

Rabbi Gilah Dror (see page 66). Today's women rabbis are treading new paths in our time, as Bruria did in hers.

chapter two

Milestones

The land that is now the State of Israel is the birthplace of Judaism and Christianity. In its capital, Jerusalem, stands the third holiest Moslem shrine. This is a land of conflicting claims and conflicting dreams, of complex political problems whose roots go back thousands of years.

Women's roles in this long and intricate history have been diverse. Women have always sustained society as mothers and keepers of the home. It was the women who passed on essential traditions to the next generation. And in every age there have been exceptional women, scholars and teachers, rulers and pioneers, who have helped shape the destiny of their peoples.

Biblical women

The Bible reveals a great deal about women, and attitudes toward women, in the ancient Middle East. In many respects, biblical society was patriarchal: men ruled and women had few legal rights. In Genesis chapter three, when Adam and Eve are punished for eating the forbidden fruit of the tree of knowledge of good and evil, Eve is told that man shall "rule over" her. Yet women played vital roles in this ancient society of mainly farmers and shepherds. Crafts made by women at home were an important part of the economy. Chapter 31 of the Book of Proverbs praises the woman who spins, weaves, buys and sells, running the household business while her husband "sits with the elders of the land."

Opposite: Women in an electronics factory. In the 1970s, women were encouraged to enter the labor force.

Right: Carpet weaving.

When It Happened

2000–1200 B.C.	Early Biblical Period	1250–1517	Mamluk rule
1200–1100 B.C.	Exodus from Egypt to Israelite settlement in the land	1517–1917	Ottoman Turkish rule
		1882	Beginning of modern Jewish immigration
1100–800 B.C.	Age of the Judges and Kings		
63 B.C.	Roman Conquest	1917–1948	British Mandate
c.4 B.C.–A.D. 32	Life and death of Jesus	1948	Establishment of the State of Israel; War of Independence
1st century	Rise of Christianity		
200–500	Development of Jewish law in the Mishna and Talmud		
		1956	Sinai Campaign
636–1099	Moslem Arab rule	1967	Six Day War
1099	Crusader conquest, slaughter of Moslems and Jews	1968–1970	War of Attrition
		1973	Yom Kippur War

Singers of songs Biblical women were not completely confined to the home. They had important roles to play in community life and some became leaders. Some scholars say that one of the ways that news and information was passed on to large numbers of people in the ancient Middle East was through the poetry and songs recited and sung by the women of that time.

Far more than being just entertainment, song played a role among the ancients similar to that of radio, TV, or newspapers today: announcing and commenting on the events of the day, expressing public opinion and social approval or disapproval. On the family and local level, songs celebrated weddings and mourned the dead. At the national level, they applauded victories and bewailed defeats. Some songs were traditional formulas passed orally from generation to generation; others were original compositions for specific events. Miriam, sister of Moses and Aaron, led the women in song and dance after the children of Israel crossed the Red Sea (Exodus 15); the Israelite women greeted David with singing and dancing when he returned from his victory over the Philistines (1 Samuel 18).

Women may have begun creating songs while spending long hours on tasks like spinning, weaving, grinding flour, baking bread, drawing water from the well. In some Middle-Eastern societies (such as the Yemenite Jews who immigrated to Israel in 1950 and earlier), women carried on the tradition of singing such "public opinion" songs into the 20th century.

Women prophets Some scholars have pointed to a connection between song and prophecy among ancient peoples, and there were indeed biblical women who reached the highest level of spiritual authority—that of prophet. Miriam was the first biblical figure, man or woman, to be designated as such. In her song of praise on the shore of the Red Sea, she expressed the important idea that it was the Lord who was responsible for the people's salvation.

An outstanding woman leader in the Bible was Deborah. Prophet, judge, and warrior, she was a powerful spiritual and political figure. Deborah is called a "mother in Israel" (Judges 5:7). Some see this as an effort to glorify the role of mother; others as an indication that her authority over the whole nation was like that of a mother over her children. Like Miriam, Deborah was a singer of songs, and the song that followed the military victory she engineered is one of the best-known in the Bible.

While four female prophets appear in the Bible—Miriam, Deborah, Hulda, and Noadiah (who lived toward the end of the period of prophecy, during the 5th century B.C.)—some scholars believe that there were others who were not mentioned by name.

> **Then Miriam the prophetess, Aaron's sister, took a timbrel in her hand, and all the women went out after her in dance with timbrels. And Miriam chanted for them, "Sing to the Lord, for He has triumphed gloriously; Horse and driver He has hurled into the sea."**
> *Exodus 15: 20, 21*

Miriam leads the women in singing and dancing.

MILESTONES 13

Women in Jewish law: gains and losses

As Jewish religious law developed gradually over the course of hundreds of years (chiefly during the 2nd to 6th centuries), there emerged attitudes toward women that differed from those of the Bible. This legal tradition, as recorded in the Mishna and the Talmud, gives women certain rights not found in the Bible (particularly in the areas of marriage, divorce, and inheritance). At the same time, women's public roles tended to diminish.

Over the course of centuries, Jewish society developed a strong tradition of learning, of scholars and sages who debated and determined the laws that regulated every area of life—and still do for Jews who observe the religious law. These scholars held the highest status in society, and this was a group from which women were almost completely excluded. Bruria (see chapter 1) was a unique exception.

Women were also exempt from the vital areas of public prayer and ritual. In the key areas of community life, then, women played a marginal role only. Their chief function was to enable their husbands and sons to participate in prayer and study. The few religious commandments that obligated women —such as lighting the Sabbath and holiday candles and the laws relating to bread-baking—centered on the family and home. Women's role in the home was glorified and their role in public life was highly restricted—a situation that, with some notable exceptions, was to prevail for centuries.

Some speak of the historical circumstances that may have helped shape this attitude. During this period of Roman rule, the Jews suffered war, forced migration, and tremendous population losses. Survival depended on home and family. As the bearers of children, women held the key not only to physical survival but also to spiritual survival: It was the women who taught children in their early years and thus passed on the tradition from generation to generation.

Certain of the patterns formed during this period affect the lives of Jewish women in Israel and elsewhere to this day. The Talmudic marriage and divorce laws apply in present-day Israel, and the traditions of the importance of women in the home and the importance of men in public life are still strong.

Women in early Christianity

Women played important roles during the lifetime of Jesus and in the early Church—more so than in the later history of Christianity.

Women were prominent among Jesus' early followers, and the Gospels present women as capable of being full-fledged disciples like men. Mary and

Martha, sisters of Lazarus of Bethany (the modern village of Al-Azariya, at the southeastern foot of the Mount of Olives in Jerusalem) are among the major women figures of the Gospels. John, chapter 11, describing the raising of Lazarus from the dead, states that "Jesus loved Martha, and her sister, and Lazarus." Martha and Mary are the only women thus singled out in the fourth Gospel.

Unusual for their time Especially interesting from the point of view of women's roles is the story of Jesus' visit to the home of Martha and Mary (Luke 10:38–42). Mary sits at Jesus' feet, to "listen to his word." Martha is busy with her duties as a hostess and asks Jesus to tell her sister to help her. Jesus answers that what Mary is doing is important: "One thing is necessary: Mary has chosen that good part, which shall not be taken away from her." He defends her right to learn, to hear God's word. This is the one thing that is necessary in life and it can thus take priority over women's traditional role of serving food—a revolutionary idea at the time (and quite different from later Church attitudes toward women).

Also unusual for their time were the women who left their homes and families and traveled with Jesus from Galilee to Jerusalem. The most important of these was Mary Magdalene, who is mentioned in all four Gospels. She was among the women who were the chief witnesses of the final events of Jesus' life, the Crucifixion, and the Resurrection.

Women were also active after the death of Jesus, in the early Christian community, as prophets, apostles, and missionaries who helped spread Christianity throughout the Roman Empire. Acts (2:17) states that both "sons and daughters" would prophesy and mentions the four daughters of Philip (21:9), who did in fact prophesy.

Women were mentioned as leaders of early Christian communities (Romans 16). Phoebe was a leader of the church at Cenchreae, Greece. Paul also mentions Priscilla and Aquila, as well as Andronicus and Junia, as missionary couples, and the latter are also called apostles (Romans 16:7).

Mary sits at Jesus' feet to learn from him; her sister Martha is anxious about serving food to the honored guest.

MILESTONES 15

Women in Islam

Starting in the 9th century, the Moslems became the predominant group in the land. With the exception of the Crusades (the holy wars fought by Christians in Palestine against Moslems during the 11th to 13th centuries), they remained so until the late 19th century. The lives of Moslem women were shaped to a great extent by the Islamic religious tradition, as well as by social and economic forces. Many of the traditions that developed during these centuries strongly affect Moslem women in Israel and elsewhere to this day.

Improvements for women Mohammed, the founder of Islam, is credited with bettering women's lives in many ways.

Moslem women praying in front of the Dome of the Rock in Jerusalem during the Ramadan holy month.

> "All people are equal, as equal as the teeth of a comb. There is no claim of merit of an Arab over a non-Arab, or of a white over a black person or of a male over a female. Only God-fearing people merit a preference with God."
> — *the prophet Mohammed*

He taught that girls should be educated along with boys, and that daughters as well as sons were entitled to inherit part of the family property. Women could earn and manage their own incomes. Parents could arrange marriages for their daughters, but were not to force them to marry someone against their will. These were all improvements over the customs that prevailed at the time. Mohammed outlawed the female infanticide that was still practiced among certain groups.

Mohammed's wives were active and independent women. His favorite, Aisha (who according to tradition was only six or seven when she was betrothed and 10 when she moved into her husband's house with her toys), was at various times a judge, a political leader and a warrior. Widowed while still a teenager, Aisha helped compile the Hadith, the sayings and teachings of Mohammed that form a major part of Islamic dogma.

But Mohammed's spirit of respect for women was not always upheld by

The Middle Eastern Family

The traditional family was an extended family. The father, his wife (or wives if he was a Moslem: Islam allows four), his children, and his married sons with their wives and children all lived in a single household—one large house or several smaller ones, often grouped around a shared courtyard in the middle. When a daughter married, she moved in with her husband's family, taking her share of the family property, if any, with her. A 1944 survey of five villages in Palestine showed that in almost 30% of the families, the married sons still lived with their parents (over 10% of the men had more than one wife).

The extended family was an economic unit. Everyone worked together on the family farm or business, which was directed by the father. Because the father owned everything, his word was law. To a great extent, the sons' wives who had joined the family were under the rule of their mother-in-law. None of the children owned any property during the father's lifetime, and they were dependent on the family business for their livelihood. This began to change in the 20th century, especially in cities where the sons could find work outside the family and become financially independent. Large mansions that had housed extended families of 30 or 40 people were divided into apartments or sold to institutions. In some villages, however, where work outside the family was scarce, the extended family economic unit lasted as late as the 1950s.

---

his followers, and over the years certain customs developed—some of them in violation of Islamic law—that placed women in a clearly inferior position.

Inferior position The birth of a son was always cause for celebration; the birth of a daughter was not. From earliest childhood, girls were trained to serve the men of the family. Although the Koran states that daughters are entitled to half the inheritance of sons (previously daughters inherited nothing), this was often ignored in practice. Sometimes brothers compensated a sister with gifts when she left the family home to marry.

According to Islamic law, the bride price (money or gifts given by the groom's family to the bride's) belonged to the bride herself and not to her father. In practice, the money often went to the father, who sometimes used it to buy jewelry or furniture for his daughter and sometimes kept it for himself.

The face veil was not required by the Koran (which states that a woman should be covered except for her face and hands), but developed as a later custom. The origins of the veil may have been more social than religious. In some areas Christian as well as Moslem women were veiled, even in the 20th century.

Winds of change The late 19th and early 20th centuries began to see some changes in women's social, legal and political status. One important impetus was closer contact with the West. The North American and European films that became popular showed how Western women lived. The growth of cities, of transportation, and of the education system also helped bring women out of isolation.

The 1917 Ottoman Law of Family Rights enacted several important changes for women. One was a minimum marriage age: 18 for boys and 17 for girls. But to avoid conflicting with Islam, which gives no lower limit for marriage, the Ottoman law allowed judges to approve marriage for a younger couple if they were mature enough (but never for girls under 9 or boys under 12). The law also restricted polygamy, restricted the husband's unlimited right to divorce his wife, and enabled women under certain conditions to divorce their husbands.

Women were given the right to vote only with the establishment of the State of Israel in 1948.

The Jewish return

Through the centuries and scattered throughout the world, the Jews maintained unique ties with their ancient homeland and with the Jewish communities that had remained there.

The last quarter of the 19th century saw the beginnings of the waves of Jewish immigration that formed the basis for the modern state of Israel.

The pioneers

In the first modern *aliya* ("ali-YA"), or immigration wave, some 25,000 East European Jews arrived in the land between 1882 and 1904. Life was difficult. It was hard to eke a living out of the stony soil. Women had to run their households with only primitive means and bear their children and treat their illnesses with little or no medical assistance.

At first most of the women immigrants retained the traditional home- and family-centered roles they had brought with them from Europe. Some worked in the fields and vineyards as well as their homes, but they were the exception rather than the rule.

At this point women in the Jewish community still had no right to vote or be elected or to be recognized as head of a household. It was only after World War I that women began to vote in the community's governing bodies.

At the same time the idea of national revival, of building a new life in the ancient homeland, had started to give women the hope for a rebirth of their own. At first this hope was expressed more in literature than in action, by women writers such as Nehama

Pukhachevski (1869–1934) and Hemda Ben Yehuda (1873–1951). Both these women were unusually educated for their time.

Hemda Ben Yehuda was married to Eliezer, the father of modern Hebrew. He saw women as crucial to reviving the ancient language, which would not truly come alive unless mothers spoke it to their children. Hemda developed this theme further, and encouraged women to educate themselves both for their own benefit and so that they would be able to teach the next generation.

Pukhachevski, Ben Yehuda, and other women writers planted seeds that were to grow during the next wave of immigration, the second *aliya*.

Women farmers

While most of the first immigration wave came in family groups, with the women following their fathers or husbands, the women of the second wave (1904–1914) were quite different. Largely 16- to 18-year-olds who came alone, on their own initiative, they were fired by ideals of creating a new, egalitarian society. These young women (representing no more than one third of all the immigrants) were almost all exceptional—in their education, in their commitment to socialist ideals, in their readiness to leave their homes in Russia or Poland and face unknown hardships in an unknown land.

These women invented a new image of the Jewish woman. They viewed physical labor, especially working the land, with an almost religious mysticism. In Palestine, however, it was at first practically impossible for women to find farming work. For the most part, they were expected to form the support system for the men—wash and mend their clothes and have their meals ready when they came back hungry from the fields.

Pioneer women farmers worked as hard as any of the men.

MILESTONES 19

The women's agricultural training farm

During the first decade of the century, the little farm work that was open to women was simply beyond their physical capacities. Most women had no choice but to support themselves through sewing, housework, and other services. Hanna Meisel (1883–1972) set out to remedy this situation.

Having studied agronomy in Europe, Meisel was the first woman in the country with a degree in agriculture. At the Sejera Collective, she and another woman had taken charge of the vegetable garden. As a result of her Sejera experience, she conceived the idea of a woman's training farm.

Meisel opened her farm on the shores of the Sea of Galilee in the spring of 1911. Her aim was to train women for agricultural work in keeping with their physical abilities; the emphasis was on dairy and chicken farming and vegetable growing. There was also a plant nursery that provided hundreds of lemon, olive, almond and eucalyptus trees to the neighboring farmers.

The students were of various ages, most about 16. They worked eight or

Manya Shochat and the Sejera Collective

When she immigrated to Palestine in 1904, Manya Wilbushewitz Shochat (1880–1961) had already worked as a carpenter, organized a workers' commune, and taken part in various radical activities in her native Russia.

Armed with her knowledge of Russian peasants and socialist ideology, Manya set out on horseback to study the situation of the Jewish agricultural workers in Palestine. She concluded that the only way they could survive was in self-sufficient farming collectives. After visiting communes in New York, Canada and elsewhere, she decided that the agricultural collective could be implemented in Palestine. "What was needed was a substitute for the religious enthusiasm that had made these [American] settlements possible, and for this substitute I looked to socialism," she wrote.

Returning to Palestine in 1907, she persuaded the authorities to lease part of an agricultural training farm at Sejera, in the Galilee, and gathered a group of 18, including several women. At that time, practically no women were doing agricultural work.

At Sejera, the women learned to plow with oxen, raise vegetables, and care for sheep and goats. Some took turns doing guard duty. At the end of its one-year contract, the collective not only avoided a deficit but even made a small profit. Short-lived but crucial, the Sejera experiment proved two important points: that the agricultural collective was feasible, thus creating a model for the kibbutz, and that Jewish women were as capable of farming work as men.

nine hours a day in the fields, orchards, and barns, and studied botany and other subjects in the evening. Except for the heavy plowing and rock-clearing, all the work was done by women.

Workers not wives The girls were very fond of Hanna Meisel, although they did not always see eye to eye. Hanna hoped her students would eventually work within a family framework, as both mothers and skillful farmers. Many of the girls did not see marriage as part of their plans; they aspired to be independent farm workers and not farmers' wives and resented the home economics part of their curriculum.

Despite the swampy ground that bred malarial mosquitos and the overcrowding that sometimes meant two girls to a bed, there was a sense of excitement and even exaltation at the farm. This was best expressed by a student, Rachel Bluwstein, who became one of Israel's best-loved poets.

Along with the rest of the country, the farm saw hard times during World War I, and was closed by budgetary problems in 1917. During its brief existence, the farm did much to change attitudes toward women working in agriculture. The farm gave women the assurance that they could produce and achieve on their own and the ability to prove that they could be valuable agricultural workers. Thanks to the training farm, vegetable growing expanded and became especially important during the food shortages of the war years, when some women formed vegetable-growing collectives. There were six such farms by 1930.

> "We were drunk with the beauty, the freedom, and the broad horizons of our new life. New, everything is so very new. The Jewish woman is a farmer...and farming is redemption."
> — *Rachel Bluwstein*

Looking after the cattle at the Nahalat Yehuda women's Agricultural Training Farm, 1926.

MILESTONES 21

The kibbutz

The socialist pioneers came with the dream of creating a new kind of community. There would be no rich, no poor, and no exploitation; everything would be equally shared. It was this dream, together with the shortage of food and work, that led to the creation of one of the world's most influential and durable experiments in collective living—the kibbutz ("ki-BOOTS," plural, kibbutzim). The first kibbutz was founded in 1910. In the early kibbutzim, small farming settlements, there was no private property whatever; even clothing was collectively owned.

> "Our women did not know how to look after babies. There was nobody whose advice Miriam [the mother] could ask. She found her own methods…wherever she went, she took the baby with her. She took him to the vegetable plots, to the kitchen, and to the poultry run. If she was in the cowshed she put him in the straw and the cow licked him."
> —*Joseph Baratz*, A Village by the Jordan, *1960*

In the first communes, the men outnumbered the women by at least three to one. The non-conformist early pioneers were not family oriented but collective oriented. The welfare of the group took precedence over any individual. At first, few married; marriage and family were rejected as reactionary. When couples did form (often without formal marriage), they were expected to treat each other publicly as they did everyone else in the group. They often did not receive time off together and were sometimes required to share their tent with a third person.

Struggling for survival, the early kibbutzim were not ready for children. A member of the first kibbutz, Joseph Baratz, recalls that when the first child was born, "everybody fussed about him and nobody knew what to do with him."

After a number of children were born, the kibbutz developed a system that allowed mothers to work and gave most of the responsibility for the children to the collective rather than to the family. From infancy, children did not live with their parents, but at a children's house, where a designated woman (but never a man) took care of them. Children spent little time with their parents, only "visiting" them between about 5 and 7 p.m. Mothers had to receive special permission to visit their babies for reasons other than breast-feeding at designated times. With some variations, this was the arrangement that prevailed at most kibbutzim until after World War II and later.

Building

While some women were struggling for the right to do farm work in the rural settlements and the kibbutz, other

Men and women work together in a kibbutz.

women in the cities were seeking the right to do other kinds of work. The renewed immigration following World War I brought more women into the cities. The British, having seized Palestine from the Turks during the war and received the United Nations (UN) mandate for the administration of the country, initiated public works projects. Most of the available jobs for newcomers were in road building. Some 400 young women worked on the highways in 1922–1923, about half of them cooking and laundering for the road crews, and half laying gravel and breaking rock.

When the public works projects began to wane, workers streamed to the cities, where most available jobs were in construction. Women learned to do floor-tiling, bricklaying, and plastering. A 1926 workers' census found 51 women tilers, 19 painters and 13 plasterers out of a total of 139 women and 2678 men in the building trades. These few dozen laborers were creating new possibilities for all women. One of them recalls spending a sleepless night after building her first wall, afraid every breeze would knock it over and ruin the reputation of all women bricklayers.

MILESTONES 23

Getting the vote

While at first the major emphasis was on the right to work, there was also a parallel movement for the right to vote. This campaign was first waged city by city and village by village, by women seeking a voice in their local governing bodies. The Tel Aviv women won the vote in 1917, and other cities followed. In 1919, women established a national suffrage organization, the Union of Hebrew Women for Equal Rights in Eretz Israel. When the Representative Assembly, the governing body for the entire Jewish community, was organized, the Union of Hebrew Women made a decision that had almost no precedent anywhere at the time: They ran an independent women's list, which won 14 seats (out of a total of 314) in the 1920 Representative Assembly elections. But women's suffrage was not formally ratified by the Representative Assembly until 1925.

When the State of Israel was established in 1948, the right to vote was extended to all men and women, Jewish and Arab.

Arms and the woman: defense

Women played an active role in the development of the Israeli military, from its earliest roots. Three women, Rachel Yanait, Esther Becker, and Manya Shochat, were members of the first Jewish defense group, organized at Sejera in 1909. Like those who plowed and laid bricks, these women were creating new roles.

A small number of young women, mostly aged 17 or 18, were active in the pre-State military organization, the Hagana, founded in 1920. Most were trained in various forms of communication: the dangerous job of carrying messages personally, working with carrier pigeons, operating radio transmitters, stringing wires for telephone connections. Women were also responsible for medical assistance.

Some women also enlisted in the Palmach, the assault companies the Hagana created for special and dangerous missions. The United Nations resolution to partition Palestine into a Jewish and an Arab state (November 29, 1947) triggered a war between the Jews and the surrounding

> "The prevailing notion was that the female member could participate in the same activities as the male member. We were trained in all areas, using the rifle, pistol, grenades, Stens, and were given physical training. We shared all the combat experiences and our effort was unbelievable."
> — *Palmach member Sarah Braverman*

A soldier in the Israel Defense Forces.

Arab countries that lasted 16 months, from December 1947 to March 1949. The Palmach units, which by that time included 1,200 women, played a crucial role in the fighting. The Palmach women served as combat soldiers, saboteurs, radio operators, drivers, and medics. Five women officers commanded combat units, remaining in service until the end of the war. Women made up one third of the convoy escorts, hiding ammunition, operating the radios, giving first aid and fighting when attacked. By 1948 women had established their right to work and to vote and their ability to take part in defense.

1948: The State of Israel is born

The establishment of the State of Israel on May 14, 1948 brought new opportunities, new challenges, and new crises. The new state very quickly established high ideals of women's equality that are still in the process of being implemented. Israel's Declaration of Independence affirms "the full social and political equality of all citizens, without distinction of religion, race, or sex." In the first Knesset (Israel's parliament), there were 11 women out of the 120 representatives (as compared to eight women today).

MILESTONES 25

Immigrant from Iraq, 1951. The immigration of Israel's early years created a complex cultural mix.

The 1949 Military Service Law obligated every woman between the ages of 18 and 34 to enlist in the army for two years. Later amendments exempted married or pregnant women, mothers, and those whose religious beliefs prevented them from serving.

Along with this progressive legislation, the early years of statehood saw a strong trend, after the years of struggle, for women to re-enter the home to raise families.

Mass immigration

Between 1948 and 1951, Israel's Jewish population doubled. Among the first immigrants were survivors of the European Holocaust. They were followed by a mass influx of Jews from Iraq, Morocco, Yemen, and other countries of North Africa and the Middle East, who completely transformed the makeup of what had been a primarily European population.

The Knesset passed several laws that had far-reaching effects on women's lives. The 1949 compulsory education law obliged parents to send both sons and daughters to school until age 14 (later extended to 15). Marriage under age 17 was prohibited. The 1951 Equal Rights Act stated equal legal status for men and women and independent property rights for married women.

In addition to rich cultures that were largely unfamiliar to the Europeans, these immigrants from Moslem countries brought with them a deeply-ingrained patriarchal tradition: Women, for the most part, had little formal education, married young, raised large families, stayed at home, and were subservient to men. Israel's compulsory education, minimum marriage age, and military service laws conflicted with this patriarchal tradition and—not without pain—gradually began to change it.

In the Arab community

Until 1948 and the early 1950s, the lives of Arab women were largely governed by long-held traditions. The disruption and trauma caused by the 1948 war and the creation of the State of Israel had far-reaching effects on Arab society in general and on women in particular.

For a variety of reasons, many people were displaced from their homes and land. Men who had formerly worked at cultivating their land had to seek a livelihood elsewhere, and their absence from the home—all day and sometimes all week—left a vacuum that was filled by women. Emerging from their traditional passive roles, women began to make family decisions that were formerly made by men. Extremely important for Arab women was Israel's compulsory education law. At first, despite the law, tradition kept most Arab families from sending their daughters to school. Arab educators worked at rebuilding the education system, and gradually parents began to send their daughters as well as their sons to school. Many of these young women became teachers, providing new role models for girls who were studying for the first time, and for women to work outside the home in other fields.

In what was probably the most significant change of this period, girls began to attend school in large numbers. The increased demand for women teachers created job opportunities, and girls' education took on economic value. Learning became a source of status for girls and their families and became central to the Arab community as a whole. (Picture shows Arab women selling their produce in Jerusalem at a bus station.)

Ora Namir

Inequality and advancement

During the 1950s and early 1960s, most of the country's energies were devoted to the task of absorbing hundreds of thousands of immigrants. While equality between men and women was on the law books, implementing this principle was not at the top of the national agenda. Public policy was directed toward creating job opportunities and occupational training, at first almost entirely for the men, the traditional breadwinners.

With the economic growth that followed the 1967 Six Day War, a labor shortage was predicted for the 1970s. Women were then encouraged to enter the labor force, especially as factory workers in food and textile plants and the new electronics industries. To enable women to work, public funds were used to build and subsidize kindergartens and day care centers. Together with private preschools, these services enabled many women to take jobs outside the home.

Following the UN declaration of 1975–1985 as the International Decade of Women, then Prime Minister Yitzhak Rabin appointed a commission, headed by Knesset member Ora Namir, to study the status of women in Israel and make recommendations "for advancing equality and partnership between men and women in all aspects of life." The Namir Commission report, published in February 1978, revealed considerable inequality in many areas. Most of its policy recommendations have yet to be implemented. Two important exceptions are the decision to institute a form of affirmative action in government service and the army's efforts to expand the range of jobs open to women (see chapter 4). The position of Prime Minister's Advisor on the Status of Women was created, but received only a tiny budget.

In 1977 Marcia Freedman, an American immigrant, organized a Women's Party to run in the coming Knesset elections. Although the party failed to receive enough votes for a Knesset seat, the organizers did succeed in bringing women's issues to public attention. Another important milestone was the creation of the Israel Women's Network (IWN). Following a 1984 dialogue with a group of American women, including such feminists as Betty Friedan and Bella Abzug, a group of Israeli women founded the IWN—a non-party lobby dedicated to making women equal partners in society. The IWN promotes legislation at the local and national levels and conducts education and consciousness-raising activities.

Under the leadership of Professor Alice Shalvi, the IWN has provided legal representation for women and addressed such issues as women in politics,

Alice Shalvi

For Israelis, the name Alice Shalvi is synonymous with feminism. A committed and observant religious Jew, Professor Shalvi sees feminism not as a break with Jewish tradition, but as a realization of its regard for the worth of every human being.

Best known as an articulate and outspoken advocate of women's rights, Professor Shalvi has made other unique contributions to Israeli society. While working as Hebrew University English literature professor and chairing the Israel Women's Network, she voluntarily served as principal of the Pelech Religious Experimental High School for Girls, making it one of Israel's finest and most innovative schools (see chapter 3).

Professor Shalvi places great emphasis on the need for sharing of responsibility both inside and outside the home. The centrality of family in Israel makes this especially important. Until men and women share work in the home—and recognize the value and worth of homemaking—we won't have equality outside the home, she says. Herself a mother of six and grandmother of many, Professor Shalvi credits her husband, Moshe, with both sharing household tasks and consistently supporting her work.

For her work on behalf of human rights, Alice Shalvi was awarded the 1989 annual prize of the Israel Civil Rights Association.

For Alice Shalvi, the early Zionist dream of creating a just society according to the vision of the biblical prophets is very much alive. She deeply believes that women can do much to make this vision a reality, if only given the chance. If it depends on Alice Shalvi, women will have this chance soon and in full.

women's health, equal opportunity, domestic violence, and women and the media. Starting in the 1980s, existing women's organizations such as Na'amat, began to take a more active women's rights position and work together with the IWN on certain issues. Universities initiated women's studies programs. A number of new groups promoting women's rights were formed, and the feminist magazine *Noga* began publication.

MILESTONES 29

Israel's Bedouin women are in transition between age-old ways and modernity.

In the Arab community

The 1970s and 1980s saw important changes for women in the Arab community.

Israel's occupation of the West Bank and Gaza Strip in the Six Day War brought the Israeli Arabs into contact with their fellow Palestinians in these areas. This interaction pointed to the importance of women's emancipation for all Palestinians and thus made it more acceptable

Two important parallel trends began to emerge: the entrance of women into the labor force and into the universities. This second trend was especially important in changing women's lives. Women students began to become involved—some even as leaders—in the politically active Arab student unions, and many joined women's associations and various ad hoc groups. Women thus became important in bringing about change in Arab society as a whole.

Women and the law

Israeli women are governed by both some of the most modern and some of the most ancient laws in the world. The modern—the civil law—is based on the principle of one law for men and women. The ancient religious laws view men and women as different, with unequal rights and obligations. The Israeli legal system gives religious law sole jurisdiction over marriage and divorce.

The religious courts Fourteen religious denominations—Jewish, Moslem, Druze and Baha'i, plus 10 Christian sects—all conduct their own religious court systems. Each denomination is responsible for marriage and divorce within its community.

Certain problems have arisen under this arrangement, particularly in the area of divorce. Under Jewish religious law, for example, a divorce is granted only if both the husband and the wife, as well as the court, agree. This has unfortunately been exploited by those who attempt to blackmail their spouses—for money, child custody, or other ends—by withholding the divorce. A large percentage of those who are blackmailed are women. Other women have been waiting many years for a divorce and

An Arab wedding. In the past it was very easy for a Moslem man to divorce his wife. Israeli civil law has made it more difficult.

cannot remarry because their husbands have deserted them or simply disappeared.

While Jewish religious law does hold solutions for those trapped in a painful state of limbo awaiting a divorce, the religious courts have so far made little use of these solutions—such as compelling the spouse who refuses to grant the divorce, through jail sentences or other means. A coalition of various women's groups and Knesset members is working hard to remedy this situation, and corrective legislation has been proposed.

According to Moslem law, a man may divorce his wife without her consent. But this "tyrannical divorce" is forbidden by Israeli civil law, and Moslem courts in Israel generally advise men against using this right.

Equality and discrimination Since its establishment, Israel has been in the vanguard of egalitarian legislation. But laws do not automatically change attitudes and practice. Although equal pay has been on the books since 1964, there is still a 30% wage gap between men and women working in the public sector. Very few discrimination cases have been brought to the courts; the procedure is expensive and time-consuming and can entail harassment from the employer. Nevertheless, encouraged by those who have sued successfully, more women are taking legal steps.

Certain laws help women remain in the work force after they have started a family.

Protective legislation Israeli women have long been proud of the laws designed to help working mothers: shorter workdays without loss of income for pregnant women; sick leave to care for children who fall ill; three months of fully-paid maternity leave for new mothers, which may be extended for another nine months without pay. The law guarantees that a woman's job will be held for her during her maternity leave and in some cases for a full year after childbirth. A 1988 amendment extended some of these benefits to fathers as well: the nine months of unpaid leave may be taken by either parent or split between them as they see fit.

In recent years, some have expressed concern that the mandatory three-month maternity leave and other benefits may discourage employers from hiring or promoting women, on the assumption that they will be absent frequently in order to care for their children. (Men, whose reserve army duty often takes them away from work for up to one or two months a year, may in fact be more prone to absence than women.)

Laws stating differential retirement ages (65 for men and 60 for women) and prohibiting night work for women have been changed. Anthropologist Naomi Nevo set an important precedent in 1990 when she won a five-year legal battle against her employer's attempt to force her to retire at age 60. Women retain the right to retire earlier and refuse night work.

A comprehensive 1988 law which prohibits discrimination in work and other areas is seen as more effective than previous legislation.

Another recent legal milestone is a June 1991 law enabling the courts to order the removal of a violent family member from the home. This has been hailed as a landmark in the struggle to protect battered spouses.

Young people in a kibbutz after a successful day in the orange groves.

The kibbutz today

The dream of the pioneers who founded the kibbutzim has in many ways become a reality. Their almost superhuman efforts have borne fruit. Swamps and deserts have become thriving communities with lush gardens and fertile fields. Kibbutz members each work according to their abilities and receive according to their needs, the classic socialist principle embodied in their daily lives. To a great extent, the experiment has worked.

The kibbutz has also evolved in ways the founding mothers and fathers did not envision.

Work At the kibbutz, women's traditional household tasks are taken care of by the collective. Meals are prepared in the communal kitchen and served in the communal dining room. Clothes are washed in the communal laundry. Preschool children are taken care of until about four in the afternoon.

Any kibbutz job, from kitchen manager to factory manager, is open to both men and women. All kibbutz members receive the same yearly budget from the collective, whether they work as kibbutz secretary (the highest administrative position) or wash the floor in the dining room.

All members are assured food, housing, medical care, and education for their children. No woman, young, old, single, married, divorced, or widowed, is dependent on a father, a husband, or any other man for economic support. Kibbutz affairs are conducted by direct democracy, with the highest authority invested in the General Assembly in which each member has one vote.

Yet the majority of kibbutz women work in jobs that parallel women's traditional tasks. Instead of doing the cooking and washing and child care for their own families, they do it for the community, in the communal kitchen, laundry, or baby nurseries. Many women also teach in the kibbutz schools. To a great extent, the traditional roles, though organized collectively, still prevail: the women take care of home, children, and education and the men take care of economics (agriculture, industry, and construction), security, and political affairs.

Family In the early kibbutzim, children belonged more to the collective than to their own parents. It was the group that was responsible for their health, education, values—their entire nurturing. Children spent almost all their waking and sleeping hours with their peers. The kibbutz has gradually restored the traditional family. A major turning point came after World War II, when many kibbutzim doubled or tripled in population. The kibbutz veterans were joined by new immigrants, many of them survivors of the European Holocaust with an intense longing for normal family life.

Parents, primarily mothers, began spending more time with their children. Families started to take responsibility for giving their children supper and putting them to bed in the children's houses where they lived. Many kibbutzim instituted the "love hour," a time when mothers visited their babies in the children's houses during the day. New mothers were given maternity leave so that they could care for their infants, and mothers of young children worked fewer hours so that they could spend time with them.

According to a 1989 survey, four times as many kibbutz women reach top-level positions as their urban sisters. Women make up 68% of kibbutz secretaries (managers). At the middle management level, such as organizing work committees, women fill 62% of the jobs. People in these positions are often responsible for handling personal problems and resolving conflicts between kibbutz members. Women fill 82% of the teaching, child care and kitchen jobs as opposed to 32% of the jobs in industry and 16% of those in agriculture.

Children are the hope and joy of Israel.

In the 1960s parents—again mainly the mothers—began pressing for their children to sleep at home rather than in the children's houses. After intense debates in individual kibbutzim and the movement as a whole, babies started sleeping at home for the first six weeks, then three to six months, then a year, and eventually, in most kibbutzim, until age 14 or 15 or even until army service at 18.

Almost always, it was the women who campaigned for a greater role in raising their children. The reasons have been hotly debated. Some maintain that the kibbutz women were simply fulfilling their biological destiny—that it is an unnatural violation of human nature for mothers to give their children over to a collective, no matter how efficient. Others argue that women were in practice denied the equal work opportunities, privileges, and obligations that were part of the socialist ideal, and that they compensated by finding refuge in their traditional roles.

Whatever the reason, the family has largely replaced the collective in raising the kibbutz children, and motherhood has high status in the kibbutz. The average kibbutz family has four or more children (five to six in the religious kibbutzim), as compared to an average of two to three in the cities.

MILESTONES 35

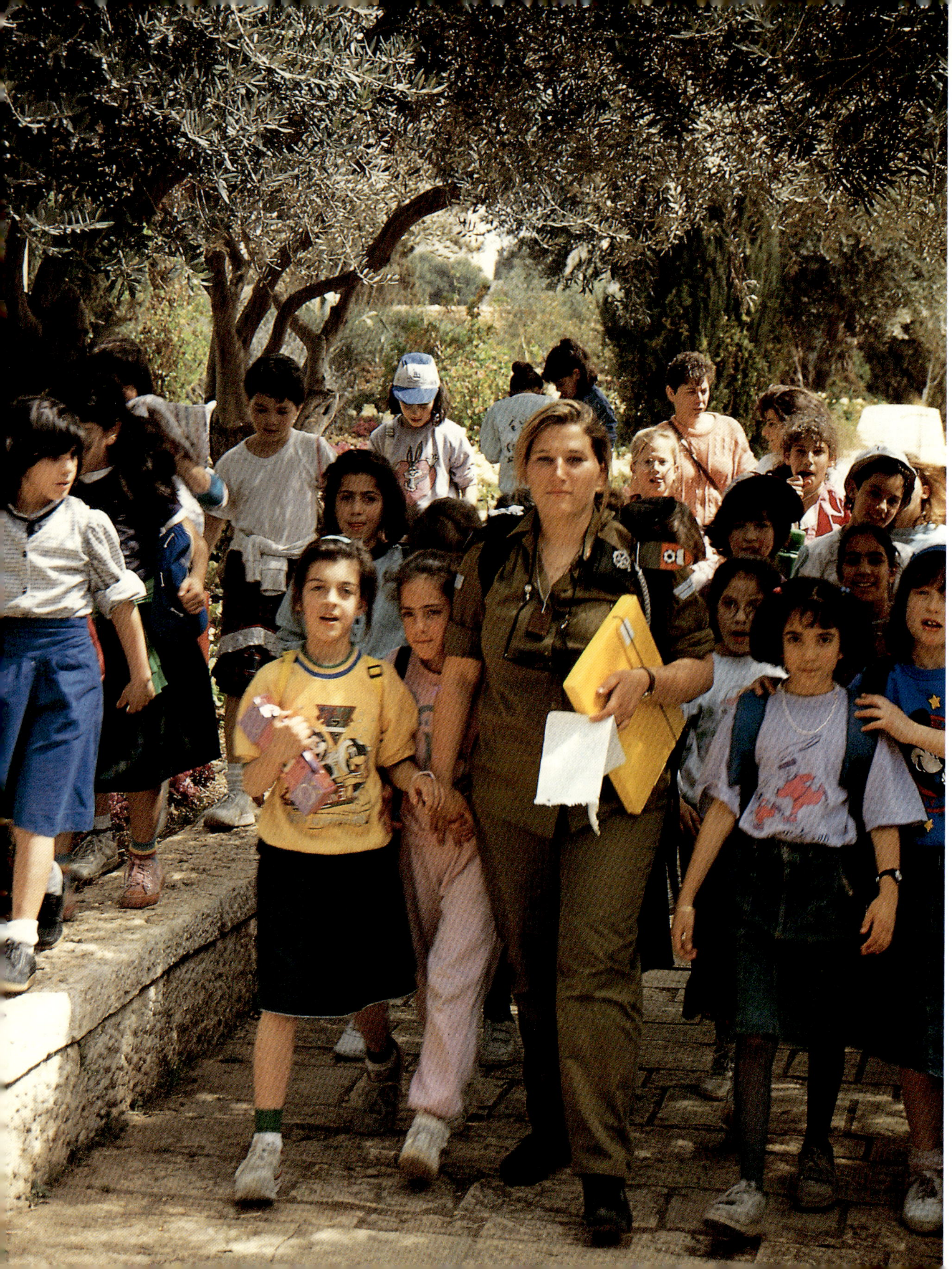

chapter three

Women in Society

In general, the growth of the economy has brought more women into the labor force, where women now constitute 40%.

Many families feel the need for two incomes. Yet family responsibilities lead many women to opt for jobs rather than careers. A large proportion of women do the clerical and secretarial work that forms the support structure for government, public services, finance, business, and other areas. At the same time, a growing number are moving into management positions. As a new country with a huge influx of new immigrants, Israel had to very quickly develop health, education, and welfare services to meet their needs. Women make up 60% of the workers in these three fields, where they have made important contributions.

Education

The Israeli education system has always faced the challenge of teaching children from many different origins and cultures. This effort continues. In September 1991, some 70,000 new immigrant pupils, most of them from the Soviet Union and Ethiopia, began attending Israeli schools. Most have been in the country less than a year and are still learning Hebrew.

Constituting 86% of the teaching staff, women are on the front lines of this endeavor, often teaching a class of 40 or more single-handedly. Some women have made outstanding contributions to the Israeli education system.

Opposite: A woman soldier with children. Jobs in the Israel Defense Forces are varied. Working with people in the community is one of them.

Right: An Arab woman at the crossroads.

The patriarch Abraham provides food for three strangers. The tradition of hospitality which originated with Abraham is shared by both Arabs and Jews.

> "Maybe you feel a little confused or embarrassed. You don't know the names of the pupils you will meet, you don't know their language, you don't know what you'll say to them. Maybe they're different from you in the way they dress, the way they talk. But remember that the Arab children are probably feeling just as shy and unsure as you are. And don't forget that there are things that all children like: games, drawing, songs, dances."
>
> — Our Neighbors and Us, *Hebrew edition, 1989*

Overcoming stereotypes Educator Yael Rom has developed remedial pre-academic programs to prepare minority-group students for university studies. Her interest in the educational problems of special groups has also been directed toward the education of girls. She believes that young women should be encouraged to overcome stereotypes and study such subjects as mathematics and engineering.

Rom speaks about women in non-traditional roles from experience: During her army service, she was the only girl in her military flying course. Rom is the only woman to have served as a pilot in the Israel Air Force. She achieved the rank of captain as pilot of a C-47 and flew combat missions during the 1956 Suez Campaign.

Our Neighbors and Us Another challenge facing Israeli schools is to combat the negative stereotypes generated by the long, complex, and bitter Arab-Israeli conflict. Every act of violence adds to the already frightening mass of prejudice.

A group of educators (all women), headed by Simcha Moses, has prepared elementary school textbooks designed to fight preconceptions and to inform. Entitled *Our Neighbors and Us*, the textbooks are published in parallel Arabic and Hebrew editions for Arab and Jewish elementary schools.

WOMEN IN SOCIETY

The Pelech Religious Experimental High School for Girls

The words "religious" and "experimental" don't usually go together. The rare combination expresses the uniqueness of this Jerusalem school.

At Pelech, girls study the Talmud and other traditional Jewish texts that in many religious schools are taught only to boys. The curriculum also includes other subjects rare in Israeli high schools: theater, women's literature, a special course on conflict resolution. Students delve into the fine points of Jewish law and put on plays by Tennessee Williams; discuss questions of prayer and religious authority and learn self-defense.

Pelech is a lively and informal place where students form strong friendships with teachers, visiting them at home and maintaining ties long after graduation. In keeping with the school's emphasis on democracy in action, everyone gathers at periodic "town meetings" where students help determine school policy. (They also take turns sweeping the school's floors.)

At many religious schools, says teacher Leah Forman Rosenthal, "there's a kind of unspoken agreement between students and teachers that the former won't raise any difficult questions and the latter won't have to deal with them. This doesn't happen at Pelech. We're investing our energy not in sweeping problems under the rug, but in facing them."

Difficult issues are dealt with: faith after the Holocaust, what Jewish tradition has to say about the conflict between Israel and her neighbors. "I don't see my role as providing pat answers, which the students may find totally inadequate in a couple years," says Rosenthal. "But we hope to help them develop the tools to deal with these complex issues in the long run. Perhaps most important, we can offer our students the assurance that they're not alone with their questions."

In one chapter, Jewish, Christian Arab and Moslem Arab children find themselves in the same hospital room and become friends. Another section discusses the various ways Arabs and Jews welcome guests into their homes. The shared tradition of hospitality is traced to the patriarch Abraham, common to the two peoples. Stories of Abraham's hospitality appear in both the Bible and the Koran. One chapter is devoted to preparing for exchange visits between Arab and Jewish schools.

Unique on the Israeli educational landscape is the Pelech Religious Experimental High School for Girls. Under the leadership of Professor Alice Shalvi (see chapter 2), who voluntarily served as principal for 15 years, Pelech gained recognition as one of the country's finest and most innovative schools.

A children's day care center organized by the Women's International Zionist Organization.

Social work

In social work, in contrast to the health and education fields, large numbers of women are active at all levels, many working as managers and administrators.

While some see this as evidence that social work is a "naturally female" profession, it may in fact have more to do with the specific history of the field in Israel. Before the birth of the state in 1948, women's organizations such as the Women's International Zionist Organization took responsibility for caring for the community's elderly, orphans, needy, and distressed. The women's groups developed a wide range of welfare services.

When the country's first welfare bureaus were established, the directors were recruited from these voluntary women's organizations. As they expanded to care for Holocaust survivors and other immigrants, the social services remained largely female, with women well represented in the senior ranks of the Welfare Ministry.

Batya Waschitz

Since she immigrated from Poland to Israel in 1941, Batya Waschitz has been working to develop the country's social services. At age 76, she hasn't stopped.

Her first jobs were with new immigrants from Syria, Kurdistan, and North Africa. Traveling from neighborhood to neighborhood by donkey, she helped families make the adjustment to a new, different, and often confusing society. Two of "her children" from those days became Knesset members.

Waschitz, who studied social work both in her native Poland and at Columbia University in New York, established and for many years directed Jerusalem's Child Welfare Department. "Working with children has always been close to my heart," she says. "In Poland, I founded and directed an orphanage. The children there were all taken to the gas chambers [in World War II]. Perhaps that's the reason I chose this kind of social work—in memory of those children whom I loved very much."

Waschitz instituted the concept of small group homes. In small group homes, children who for various reasons could not live with their families are cared for in family-like settings instead of impersonal large institutions. She promoted treatment of the entire family, so that in time the children could return to their homes.

When she retired five years ago as director of Jerusalem's Social Services Department, Waschitz embarked on a new career as a full-time volunteer. The day after she left her office, she started working at "A Listening Ear," a telephone hotline for teenagers which she established. Soon after, she began organizing support groups, a telephone hotline, and a crisis intervention center for Russian and Ethiopian immigrants. She has learned Russian and recently visited the Soviet Union to help prospective immigrants prepare for their move to Israel. "As long as I have the strength, I will continue to work, to organize, and to study," says Waschitz.

Immigrant absorption

The Hebrew word for immigrants is *olim* ("oh-LIM")—literally meaning those who go up. In Jewish tradition, people who move to Israel are seen as ascending—achieving what has always been a national ideal. But "going up" to Israel means moving to a complex, turbulent, and, for the newcomer, often bewildering country. A major Israeli activity is thus "absorption"—the process of helping immigrants find their way in their new home, involving everything from Hebrew language teaching to shopping assistance to trying to explain Israeli politics. As both professionals and volunteers, women do the lion's share of this work.

As important as the government absorption bodies are the immigrants' neighbors. In this capacity woman have done a great deal. Some belong to organized volunteer groups; others simply open their doors and greet the immigrant families who move in next door with a smile and a cake.

Absorption volunteers

Among the many volunteer groups organized to help the *olim*, Keren Klita, a Jerusalem aid group for Russian immigrants, has become a model. Initiated by Delysia Jayson, herself an immigrant from England, the group is operated largely by women. Among Jerusalem's many attractions for new immigrants is Keren Klita's reputation for warm and efficient assistance.

Keren Klita tries to match every new Russian family—over 6,000 now live in Jerusalem—with a veteran Israeli, someone who can offer friendship and help in surmounting the countless quandaries facing the newcomer: dealing with unfamiliar banks and post offices, finding the best schools, locating a doctor at midnight, dealing with the innumerable pieces of bureaucratic paper that are part of the first weeks in a new country. Over 1,000 volunteers are involved. Keren Klita, funded solely by contributions, also provides each new family with a "welcome basket" of basic food and household supplies, and when possible, cooperates with overstrained government agencies in meeting special needs, such as providing medical equipment.

The women who run Keren Klita are smart, serious, dedicated, and organized—volunteers who work like professionals. Many have large families or work full time or both. Volunteer Frances Wolff says, "There's nothing small about the organization, no sense of anyone wanting personal credit for anything—just a concerted effort to get the job done." Many are religious women; all of them believe the common good has an important claim on their time and energy. They see the Soviet immigrants as a human treasury of talent and resourcefulness with the potential to contribute vastly to Israeli society. Says Frances Wolff, who in addition to raising eight children invests numberless hours in Keren Klita, "The main reward is just getting to know these people."

Hebrew language teaching

Over the past 100 years, Hebrew has emerged from the Bible and the prayer book to become the daily language of Israelis originating from different countries. Immigrants speaking a babel of tongues have learned Hebrew in a network of *ulpan* ("ul-PAN" intensive language teaching) programs throughout the country. The great majority of the teachers are women.

Shulamit Katznelson and Ulpan Akiva

Under the dynamic leadership of Shulamit Katznelson, students from 122 countries have learned Hebrew at Ulpan Akiva in Netanya. People from some 20 different countries study there every month. In addition to its Hebrew programs for immigrants, visitors and diplomats, Ulpan Akiva runs Arabic courses for Jewish Israelis and Hebrew programs for Arab Israelis.

The courses are residential, giving Arabs and Jews a rare chance to eat, sleep and study together. At a short Arabic course for Knesset members, these politician-students drove to Jerusalem every afternoon to vote and returned at night to have coffee with Arab and Druze alumni of the *ulpan* and Ali Yehia Adib, director of the Arabic program.

"Friendships were formed in those 17 days, and some problems were solved through short cuts created by these friendships," says Katznelson. "We are not naive politically, and we know that we at Ulpan Akiva are not the ones who are going to make peace in the region. But unpredictable things happen here; we create a meeting place." For their creative teaching and for creating this meeting place, Shulamit Katznelson and the staff of Ulpan Akiva were awarded the Israel Prize for education, the country's highest tribute, in 1986. Shulamit Katznelson was recently nominated for the Nobel Peace Prize.

WOMEN IN SOCIETY

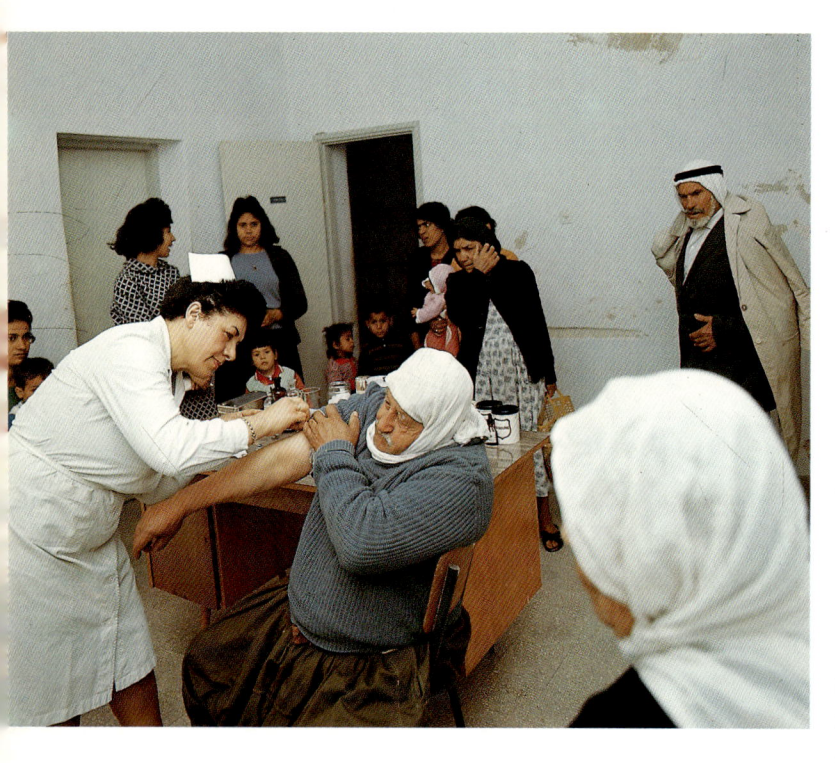

Women work in a wide range of jobs in Israel's health services.

Medicine

Many of Israel's doctors—half of all health clinic doctors—are women. Many have made important contributions.

Dr. Naomi Amir, a native of Chicago, established Israel's first department of pediatric neurology, at Jerusalem's Bikur Holim Hospital. At the Spafford Children's Hospital in East Jerusalem, she treats children who come to the hospital from throughout the Arab world. "I fully believe that it is people who live together, even if governments don't always see eye to eye," she says. "I use my profession to bring people together."

Dr. Atara Kaplan De-Nour, Professor of Psychiatry at Jerusalem's Hadassah-Hebrew University Medical Center, became the first woman to chair a department at Hadassah when she was appointed head of psychiatry in 1982. She is especially interested in the psychological problems of the physically ill and the security situation as a major source of stress for the Israeli population. "The inability of Israelis to plan the next day, the next week, and the next year causes great stress. People react to insecurity by becoming aggressive and by concentrating on the here and now."

Hematology Professor Dr. Bracha Ramot has done pioneering work at several Israeli hospitals. Part of her work is helping patients cope with cancer: "I always tell my patients the truth," she says. "But like any truth, you can look at the half empty glass or the half full glass. I try to encourage my patients to fight."

Since a large number of women doctors are also mothers, many choose such specialties as internal medicine rather than those requiring emergency work at night. Family medicine, a fairly new specialty in Israel, is attracting many women doctors. A recent family medicine course was attended entirely by women.

Another exceptional woman is Dr. Renee Hana, one of Israel's five women general surgeons. For her, every day brings another drama: all-night surgery to save a five-year-old hurt in a car crash; eight victims of a terrorist shooting rushed into the emergency room. Dr. Renee, as she's known to her colleagues, is part of a tiny elite. As a Christian Arab from a small Galilee village, she is unique.

The will to work hard and achieve, says Dr. Hana, came with the air she breathed at home. "For almost everyone in the village, education was at the center of life—more important than money, more important than honor, more important than politics." Dr. Hana, 33, remembers herself as a serious child who read all the time. Even her mother, a first grade teacher, said she swallowed books like a worm.

Her earliest ambitions were to become a writer or an architect, and she spent several months studying civil engineering before starting medical school in Jerusalem. Dr. Hana remembers the first years of struggling with unfamiliar material in an unfamiliar language as a near nightmare. "I had terrible regrets; it was only the fear of admitting failure that kept me going." The turning point came when medical theory connected to practice, to healing real people. "The day I learned to use a stethoscope was when I began falling in love with medicine," she says.

Despite the 12-hour days, the sleepless nights, the constant emotional and physical pressure, Dr. Hana thinks surgery is a good profession for women. She sees the capacity for precise and delicate work and for functioning effectively despite fatigue as women's qualities that suit the job.

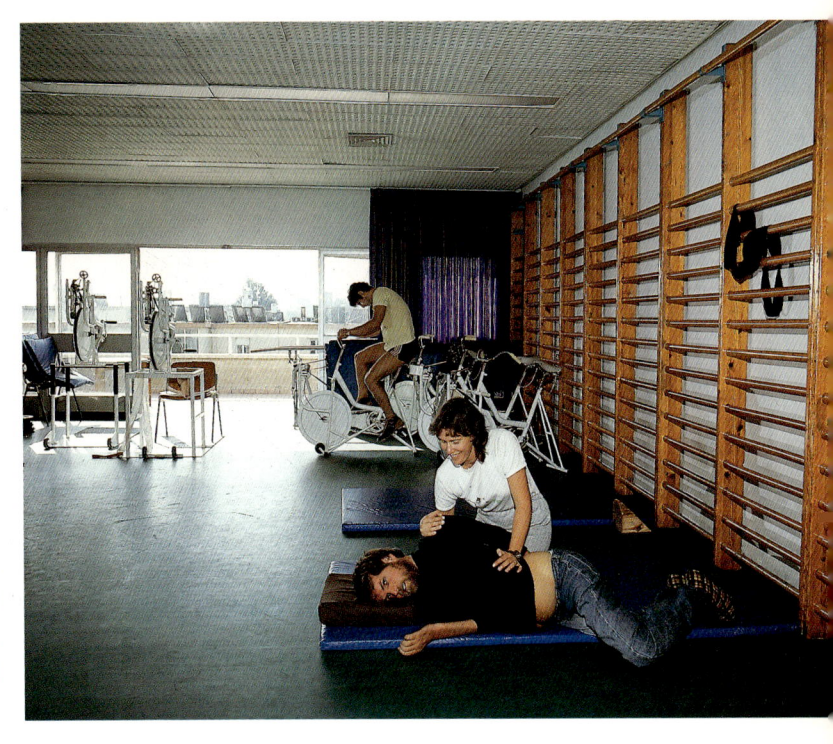

Paradoxically, Dr. Hana's achievements have placed her in a kind of no man's—or no woman's—land between Israel's Arab and Jewish societies. It is hard for her to envision herself in a traditional Arab marriage, subservient to a man. Marrying a Jew seems equally unlikely. She cannot imagine returning to her native village. "My personal situation is a bit complicated," she says.

A physical therapist works with an injured soldier at a rehabilitation center.

WOMEN IN SOCIETY 45

State Attorney Dorit Beinish (seated) in Israel's Supreme Court

> "My progress was, I believe, quite natural, quite normal. I do not consider myself a career woman. I did not plan any career for myself. I simply did whatever job I had to do. I don't believe I had any ambitions as far as advancement in the Justice Ministry was concerned."
> — *Yehudit Karp, Deputy State Attorney*

Law

Close to 30% of Israel's lawyers are women. As men trained in law have increasingly entered the lucrative private sector, women have been filling important governmental posts. State Attorney Dorit Beinish and Deputy State Attorney Yehudit Karp are two prominent examples; most of the lawyers in the State Attorney's Office are women. Many women serve as judges. Law Professor Ruth Lapidot has been a member of the Israeli delegation to the United Nations and participated in the final stages of the 1979 peace negotiations between Israel and Egypt. She recalls the signing of the treaty in Washington, DC as one of the "great moments" of her life.

"I like law because I like its logic," says Professor Lapidot. "Law is a technique of the social sciences. It is not an end in itself, but a means to improve the social environment. I like an academic career because I like the academic freedom of a university and the flexible time schedule that permits me to combine my work with my family responsibilities."

WOMEN IN SOCIETY

In 1989 Ghada Sa'ad was appointed Traffic Court judge at the Magistrate's Court in her native Nazareth, becoming the first Arab woman to serve as a judge. After graduating from the Nazareth Baptist High School and the local public high school, Ghada Sa'ad had planned to study psychology. But a family friend persuaded her to study law at the Hebrew University in Jerusalem.

"I could never have achieved what I have without the support and help I received from my husband and family," she says. "My parents and my mother-in-law have looked after our three children and the home. My mother-in-law, who lives in the apartment below ours, does all the cooking, leaving me free to prepare cases and study new aspects of law at home."

Ghada Sa'ad began law school in Jerusalem when she was 17. She had never left home before. Studying law was at first extremely difficult for her. One of the hardest parts was studying in Hebrew rather than her native Arabic. And at that time, Ghada's community still looked somewhat askance at university studies for girls. Most families hoped to see their daughters get married right after high school. Ghada's parents, however, supported her decision. When she called home during her first months at the university, telling her parents that she wanted to quit and come home, it was they who told her that all beginnings were difficult and encouraged her to continue.

Miriam Ben-Porat

Miriam Ben-Porat, 73, has been called "the first lady of Israeli law." She was the first woman appointed to the Supreme Court, where she served as deputy president and laid down important legal precedents. Now serving as State Comptroller, responsible for investigating the workings of the government, she has given the position new importance and visibility. Many Israelis have come to see her as the champion of morality in the country's political life. "I cannot recall any state comptroller who has been as popular as Ben-Porat," said one Knesset member. In a recent magazine poll, she was elected "Man(!) of the Year."

Miriam Ben-Porat is known for both her courage and her objectivity. Said a prominent lawyer who once clerked for her, "If she is uncertain about a matter, she will delve into it until she is convinced she has found the truth."

"My judicial experience is invaluable in helping me carry out my duties [as State Comptroller]," says Ben-Porat. "A judge's approach has to include upholding the law on the one hand and love of one's fellow human beings on the other. I think I've brought that combination with me to this work."

For her work in developing Israeli law and preserving the rule of law, Miriam Ben-Porat was awarded the 1991 Israel Prize, the highest national award.

Politics

Israel is one of very few countries worldwide that has had a female head of state—Golda Meir, who in 1969 became Israel's fourth prime minister. Yet Golda, as everyone called her, was a rare exception. Since the founding of the state in 1948, only a small handful of women have served as government ministers. In the current Knesset (Israel's parliament), eight out of the 120 members are women—6.6 %. This is slightly higher than the U.S., where 5% of the Congress are women, but much lower than countries such as Norway, Finland and Sweden, where women make up over 30% of the parliaments.

Lasting impressions Although modest in number, Israel's women Knesset members have made—and are making—their mark on the country's political scene. Two of these women, representing opposite sides of the political spectrum—Geula Cohen on the right and Shulamit Aloni on the left—founded their own political parties. Knesset member (MK) Sara Doron leads the Knesset faction of the Likud, one of the country's two largest parties.

On the whole, the women MKs have been notably successful in initiating legislation and getting it passed. Labor MK Shoshana Arbelli-Almozlino, who now chairs the Knesset Economics Committee, has been particularly active in this regard. For the most part, the women MKs have concentrated on the areas of health, education, and welfare, rather than security and foreign affairs.

In their ability, determination, and capacity for hard work, these women are all exceptional—for it is not easy for a woman to enter Israeli politics. Family holds high priority for most Israeli women, and family and politics do not easily mix. Arbelli-Almozlino, born in in Iraq in 1926 and a Knesset member since 1966, said in a 1989 interview, "Most women who want a career choose a profession. Politics is all-consuming.

Geula Cohen in the Knesset.

One has to devote oneself to it entirely and sacrifice everything else."

High barriers The typical routes to political office are largely closed to women. One path is working one's way up through the party, which in the Israeli political system wields considerable power. Voters choose parties rather than individual candidates. It is the parties that place their candidates higher or lower on their lists, determining which stand a realistic chance of getting a Knesset seat. (For example, if party X wins 10 seats, candidates numbered 11 and down are out.)

The party route is problematic for women. Sometimes women begin working for a party before their children are born and drop out for 10 or 15 years while they are raising children and probably holding down a job at the same time. If they return to the party when their children are older, they are likely to be asked where they were all those years—the years when their male fellow party members have been busily establishing names for themselves.

Another path to politics is through the army—especially through leadership in combat units. But while women bear increasingly serious responsibility in the Israel Defense Forces, they do not engage in combat and relatively few women choose the army as a career. So this path is also largely closed to women.

How do women enter politics? One road is through women's organizations, especially the Na'amat labor organization, the largest women's group in Israel. Many of Na'amat's leaders have gone on to local or national politics. Labor MK Ora Namir, herself a former secretary of Na'amat's Tel Aviv branch, says that "without Na'amat we would have fewer women in politics." Another way is all-women's lists. In 1977, such a list did constitute a party. While this tactic has not been successful on the national scene, it has at times worked in local politics. In the 1989 municipal elections, the women's movement of the National Religious Party ran its own all-women's list (in this case, not a party but an ad hoc group) for the Jerusalem City Council. The group won one seat, occupied by Yehudit Huebner, formerly Israel's ambassador to Norway.

Shulamit Aloni in the Knesset. There aren't many women in the Knesset, but they are a presence to be reckoned with.

WOMEN IN SOCIETY

And even higher If tall barriers surround the political world for Jewish women, for Arab women they are almost insurmountable.

While a growing number of Arab women are stepping out of traditional roles to become doctors, lawyers, journalists, and educators, politics poses special problems. The very essence of political life—meeting with men, arguing with men, expressing opinions without deferring to men—runs directly counter to the traditions of proper women's behavior that are still very strong. Says psychologist and educator Nabila Espanioly: "In Arab society, leading is something that men do."

Despite all this, a small number of exceptional Arab women have chosen to make their way into political life. One pioneer was the late Violet Khoury, the first Israeli Arab woman to hold elective office (see chapter 4). Samia Hakim, who holds a seat on the Nazareth city council, is another. Hakim is used to breaking new ground. When she opened her own hairdressing salon 30 years ago, there was only one other woman in Nazareth who ran her own business. "I had to fight with my husband, with my family, with society," she recalls. "The issue was, how can a woman be outside the home, dealing with men?" Islamic movement members of the Nazareth city council have objected to a woman debating with men in public, but Hakim stood her ground.

Alice Shufani, a Christian Arab from a small village in the western Galilee, was elected to the central committee of the Mapam party only a year and a half after she joined the party.

Rola Mantzur, 25, is also active in Mapam and serves as secretary of the Na'amat branch in her native village of Taibe. Mantzur says it was her mother, denied the chance to study herself, who encouraged her to study Arabic literature and Middle Eastern history at Tel Aviv University. Ten to 15 years ago there wasn't a single university-educated woman in Taibe, says Mantzur; today there are five or six doctors. In addition, a number of Arab women are active in the Israeli Communist party.

Theater

Many of the great ladies of the Israeli theater immigrated to Israel and began appearing on stage while they were still learning Hebrew.

Miriam Zohar was born in Rumania and at age 12 was sent to a Nazi forced labor camp in the Ukraine. After World War II ended, she wandered through Rumania and Hungary and in 1948 joined a group of immigrants sailing for Palestine. When they arrived in Haifa harbor, all the passengers were sent by the British, who then ruled the country, to a detention camp in Cyprus. It was there that Zohar first performed, in amateur outdoor productions organized by refugee relief groups.

In Israel, Zohar first appeared with an immigrant theater group performing in Yiddish. Soon she was asked to join the Habimah National Theater Company. Miriam Zohar has starred in such plays as *A Long Day's Journey Into Night*, *The Miracle Worker*, and *Who's Afraid of Virginia Woolf*. Among her most memorable roles was Hannah Senesh (see chapter 5) in the stage version of her story.

Lea Koenig was born in Poland in 1931 and first acted in the Jewish National Theater of Bucharest, Rumania. She immigrated to Israel in 1961 and began performing with Habimah five months after her arrival, while she was still learning Hebrew.

Orna Porat has been appearing on the Israeli stage since she immigrated from her native Germany in 1947. Her belief that children of all ages deserve quality theater led her to found Israel's Children and Youth Theater.

Porat starred in the Hebrew stage version of *Driving Miss Daisy*. The role was one of her favorites: "Daisy is stubborn, opinionated, impossible, but likeable—like me."

A performance of Lorca's "Blood Wedding" performed by the Chamber Theater in 1970 with Orna Porat (right) as the mother.

WOMEN IN SOCIETY   51

"A weird, happy ending" Hanna Marron, one of Israel's most popular actresses, was born in Germany in 1923 and began performing on stage at age four. Her family immigrated to Israel in 1933 when Hitler came to power.

In her 50 years on the stage, Marron has appeared in roles ranging from Shakespeare to modern Hebrew drama to *Hello Dolly*. "I am for entertainment," she says, "but it must be good quality. The theater must act as the herald of its society; it must have a message." Marron has appeared in a popular television series which she feels did carry such a message beyond the fun and humor. While she did find the popular level of TV as compared to the stage problematic, she saw the program as a way of reaching an audience that rarely goes to the theater.

In 1970 Marron was badly wounded in an Arab terrorist attack at the Munich airport. Her left leg had to be amputated to save her life. Marron says it was the flood of mail and outpouring of love from Israel that gave her the courage to go on. She especially remembers a letter from a young soldier who himself lost both legs: "Dear Hanna, you're wounded and people will tell you not to pay attention, that everything will be all right. Well, nothing will be all right You'll never be as you were before. But if you want to, you can be different and even better. I want to see you on stage when you come back." Marron returned to the stage, found the soldier, and invited him to her first performance after her recovery. "Later he got married and we danced together at his wedding," she recalls. "It was kind of a weird, happy ending."

"What happened to me has not made me hate those who did it," says Marron. "I don't love the people who did it. I was also sorry that the Germans let them go free. But it's not a matter of hatred, rather of trying to understand the other side. At the same time, I won't accept that violence is the way to achieve a goal."

In 1989 Marron participated in a Brussels conference of Palestinian and Israeli women entitled "Give Peace a Chance—Women Speak Out."

"I believe in dialogue," she says. "Even though it may have taken years, there are many places around the world where conflicts have been solved. Only don't allow weapons to be put in the hands of extremists!"

> **"When I prepare myself for a role, I study the character from all points of view. It does not make life easy, because I always see many aspects at the same time. This approach also works off stage."**
> *— Hanna Marron*

Sports

When she returned from the Barcelona World Judo Championships with a third-place bronze medal in July 1991, Yael Arad immediately began preparing to return to Barcelona a year later for the 25th Olympic games.

"I started judo by chance when I was eight, because my brothers used to do judo. People thought I was crazy, a young girl getting up early to train," she says. Arad won her first national championship at 10 and took second place in the junior world championships when she was 16.

"I love the mysticism, the technique, the magic of judo," says Arad. "For me, it's an art where I can express myself individually through nuances of movement and technique."

Doing her best After her army service, Arad began studying for a degree in nutrition, but the pressures of training forced her to postpone regular study. "I have a close circle of friends," she says, "and I never let judo interrupt my social life to the extent that I become a recluse." Looking forward to the 1992 Olympics, Arad says that "the issue for me is not about medals but about reaching my peak. In order to do better than third place, I will have to beat Britain's Diane Bell, who defeated me in Barcelona." Yael Arad was selected as Israel's 1991 Sportswoman of the Year.

Yael Arad says, "I'm a very proud Israeli and I feel wonderful when I see our flag raised at an international meet. I still haven't worked out just where the line is dividing personal and national success. Am I winning for me or for Israel? I think the bottom line is that I love success, but it's a success that comes through hard work and individual effort."

Broad-jumoer Tami Levy in action, 1991.

WOMEN IN SOCIETY 53

Esther Shachamorov Roth One of the country's most celebrated athletes, Esther Shachamorov Roth is Israel's greatest track and field star. When she was 14, Esther tried out with coach Amitzur Shapira and at their first meeting beat him in the 60 meter dash. From that day on, they worked together constantly. An all-round athlete, Esther specialized in hurdles, which combine speed, strength, and agility. Starting in 1970, Esther and Amitzur Shapira embarked on an intensive training program with one goal in mind—the 1972 Munich Olympics.

"When we came to Munich, I was only 19 and spent the first few days there in a state of shock," recalls Esther. "It was like nothing I had ever seen before, with thousands of athletes from all over the world." Esther qualified for the semi-finals in the 100-meter hurdles.

Israel's 1989 record-holder in the women's 400-meter race, Iris Gilad.

"I remember so well Amitzur hugging me at the end of the heat and saying, 'Esther, you've just made me the happiest man in the world.' I was the only one on the Israeli team still competing, and the whole team rallied around me. We had become a tightly-knit family, and spirits were sky-high."

Esther never ran in the hurdles event. The following day, September 5, Amitzur Shapira and 10 other Israeli team members were killed by Arab terrorists. "Peace, brotherhood, the Olympic spirit—all these exploded in front of my eyes," says Esther. "I had no desire to return to the athletics arena. I never really got over Munich, and every race from then on reminded me of 1972."

Eventually persuaded to return to competition, Esther won three gold medals in the 1974 Asian Games and entered the 1976 Montreal Olympics "with a feeling of unfinished business from Munich." There she became the first Israeli to enter the finals of an Olympic event and took sixth place in the 100-meter hurdles.

Esther trained for the 1980 Moscow Olympics, but after Israel joined 65 Western countries in boycotting the games in protest over the Soviet invasion of Afghanistan, she retired from competitive athletics. Now working as a physical education teacher and raising two children, she still finds time to play tennis and basketball, to swim—and to run.

Table tennis champion Tatianna Shtobles, a new immigrant from the then Soviet Union, 1991.

Balls or Dolls? The total number of Israeli men competing in six leading sports—basketball, tennis, volleyball, swimming, track and field, and gymnastics—is about 33,000. The total for women in these sports is just over 13,000. (Another 35,000 men play competitive soccer, the country's most popular sport, in which women do not participate.) Why the gap? Some say men are simply more interested in sports; others charge that nothing is done to promote women's sports: They get less financial support, less TV coverage, and inferior training conditions. Lakhen, the Organization for the Advancement of Women's Basketball and Sports, is working to remedy this. "It all starts when the baby boy is given a ball and the girl a doll," says Orna Ostfeld, head of Lakhen.

"Boys' participation in sports is seen as legitimate; girls' is not." One of Lakhen's victories has been improved training facilities for the women's national basketball team—an investment that has proved itself. In June 1991, the team competed in the women's European National Basketball Finals. "Women have to learn to fight," says Anat Dreigur, captain of the team. "Everything that women have won until now, they have won by themselves. Nothing has been given to us."

WOMEN IN SOCIETY

A student learning Arabic. Advancement of instruction in Arabic language and literature is one of the programs in the education system.

Literature

Although few knew Hebrew before the turn of the century, women have made important contributions to Israeli literature from its beginnings. For the most part, women's writing has been lyrical—expressing personal feeling and individual experience, the "I" rather than the "we." Men, on the other hand, have tended to write about the collective national experience, the epic dramas of the founding of the country, the conflicts, and the wars.

Writer Amalia Kahana-Carmon says that women have been seen as "sensitive observers of small details, writing about domestic and romantic issues," and thus some have viewed women writers as marginal. But the personal writing women have been producing has recently received much serious attention, and the past few years have seen a wave of new women's writing. While until recently most women writers have been poets, many are now writing novels and short stories.

Different experiences Writer Savyon Liebrecht, one of these important new voices, speaks of the difference between the writers who came of age around 1948, when the state was founded, and her own generation, born at that time: "Then the central Israeli experience was war, and women were largely excluded from that. Now the central Israeli issues are available to both male and female writers: the conflicts between Arabs and Israelis, the way Holocaust survivors have rebuilt their lives here in Israel, the conflicts between the religious and the non-religious."

In *Apples from the Desert*, Liebrecht writes of an 18-year-old girl who runs away from her strictly religious home to live with a boy on a secular kibbutz. When her mother travels to the kibbutz to "bring her back by the hair," mother and daughter talk to each other openly for the first time. On one level the story is about love and the absence of love between husband and wife, parents and children. On another, it is about the separations and connections between two different Israeli worlds—a traditional Jerusalem neighborhood and a non-religious kibbutz in the desert.

From poetry to novels One of Israel's most important and prolific writers is Shulamit Lapid. "I always wrote," says Lapid, 58. "I wrote poetry when I was younger. Later I thought it was a caprice of the young, so I threw out hundreds of poems. My first book was published when I was 35—very late for any writer." She quotes another writer, Shulamit Hareven, who said that "when the children are small, we [women] write poetry. When they grow up, we write short stories. When they leave home, we write novels."

Lapid's historical novel *Gai Oni* (*Valley of My Strength*) was a runaway best-seller in Israel. Fanya, the 16-year-old heroine, arrives in Palestine in the 1880s after her family is killed in a pogrom in Russia. She struggles against hunger, cold, and misery to stay alive in a tiny farm settlement in the Galilee, eventually discovering a new identity as a Jew and as a woman.

"I was fascinated with those early settlers and felt we never had a true picture of them," says Lapid. "For some reason, this story really appealed to readers. Feminists were taken with Fanya's story, and many people apparently found it enlightening. That was one of the things I hoped to accomplish—to give Israelis a sense that their country wasn't entirely born in 1948." Readers were moved by Fanya's hard-earned courage and endurance and some even visited the town where the story took place to look for the grave of the totally fictional character.

From 1983 to 1987, Lapid chaired the Israel Writers' Association. "After I had sat for six years in my room and met nobody—that was the time when I had written one book after another—I felt a great urge to get in touch with life again, so I offered my name for the position of chairwoman. If you're a good writer, you're accepted here in Israel, whether you're male or female," says Lapid. "I write mostly about women. I feel more deeply for their plight. I used to write a lot about women who do men's work, to change the image of women in society. But now I don't try to change society, I try to depict it."

Women reading in a library.

WOMEN IN SOCIETY

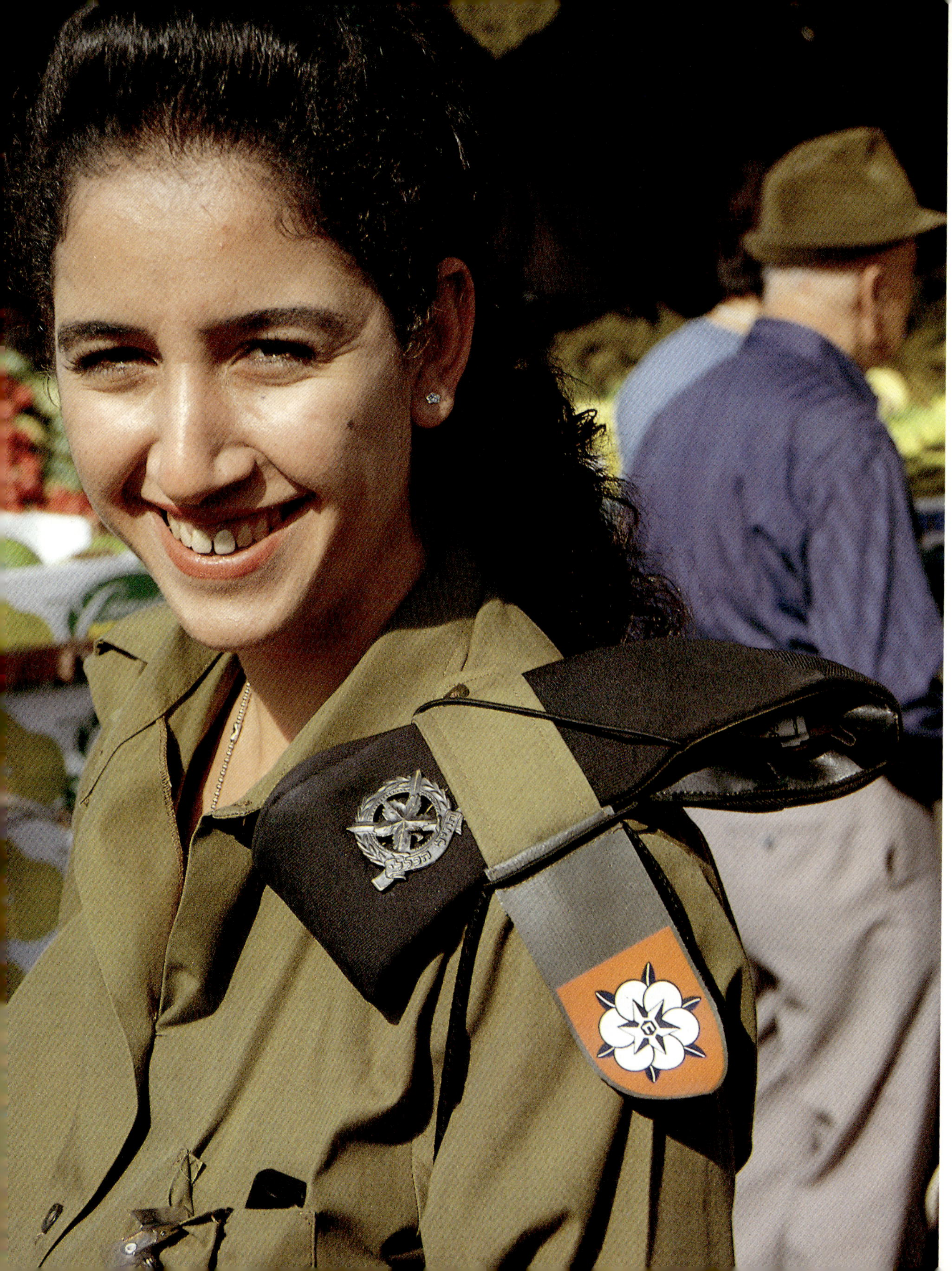

chapter four

Being Woman

Israeli women face many of the same issues that, in one way or another, confront their sisters around the world: equal opportunity, political representation, division of responsibility at home, the unsolved problems of work and family in women's lives. As in many other countries, men's and women's conventional roles are being challenged and are changing in ways that are not yet completely clear.

At the same time, certain distinctive circumstances shape the lives of Israeli women. In this chapter, we will look at three of them: Immigration, the mixture of people from over 50 different countries, all with their own cultures and attitudes toward women's roles; Traditions and Transitions, the various religious and social customs that shape women's lives and how they are changing; and War and Peace, the prolonged and painful Arab–Israeli conflict and how it affects all Israeli women.

Opposite: A soldier in the Israel Defense Forces. Women in the army have recently moved into jobs traditionally done by men.

Right: An Arab school girl on a school excursion. This would have been a rare sight in the past.

Immigration

Israel is a country of immigrants. From the 400,000 North African and Middle Eastern Jews who streamed into the country between 1948 and 1951 to the recent Soviet and Ethiopian newcomers, each group has brought new skills, new customs, new ideas. Each new group has both enriched and challenged those already living in the country—many of them immigrants themselves. Immigration continues today. In 1990 alone, close to 200,000 persons immigrated to Israel.

A Yemenite Jew born in Israel.

The Yemenites

The majority of the Yemenite Jewish community arrived in Israel between June 1949 and June 1950, in a mass airlift known as "Operation Magic Carpet." Several thousand others had earlier made the dangerous trek across the Arabian desert on foot or by caravan. Many of them perished along the way. The Yemenite Jews brought rich and varied traditions of music, dance, crafts, and celebrations related to marriage, some of which are still practiced (see chapter 6). Among Yemenite women, the tradition of caring for others in the community is strong, as is the tradition of song.

Israelis' countries of origin (partial list): Albania, Algeria, Argentina, Austria, Belgium, Brazil, Bulgaria, Canada, Chile, China, Colombia, Cuba, Czechoslovakia, Egypt, England, Ethiopia, France, Germany, Greece, Holland, Hungary, India, Iran, Iraq, Italy, Libya, Mexico, Morocco, Poland, Rumania, Russia, South Africa, Southern Yemen, Spain, Sweden, Switzerland, Tunisia, Turkey, United States of America, Uruguay, Venezuela, Vietnam, Yemen, Yugoslavia

Helping others One of the outstanding women of the Yemenite community is Rabbanit Bracha Kapach. Married according to Yemenite custom at age 11 and a mother at 14, Rabbanit Kapach has become a one-woman social welfare agency in her Jerusalem neighborhood. Her favorite biblical verse—"You shall love your neighbor as yourself" (Matthew 22:39)—is no mere sentiment but a call to action. It was during her childhood in Yemen that she learned the habit of attending to the needy. The highest form of giving was to give in secret, without the recipients' knowledge.

From her home, Rabbanit Kapach dispenses advice and support, organizes various forms of financial assistance, and distributes holiday food packages to hundreds of needy families. She has organized literacy classes for women who never went to school and vacations for hardworking mothers of 10 children or more. Rabbanit Kapach has been honored with the Jerusalem Good Citizenship award and other tributes, but her chief reward, she says, is in fulfilling the biblical commandments. "That's what gives me stamina, good health, and the desire to live. For me, that is enough."

Ofra Haza

Perhaps more than any other group, the Yemenites have shaped the sound of contemporary Israeli music. International singing star Ofra Haza is carrying on a long tradition exemplified by such earlier Yemenite women singers as Bracha Zefira and Shoshana Damari (see chapter 5).

Haza, 31, is the youngest of nine children of Shoshana and Yefet Haza, who in the 1930s made their way from El Haz in Yemen to Palestine by foot. She remembers her childhood in Tel Aviv with great warmth. The neighborhood was like an extended family, and she would carry platters of her mother's food to needy families every Friday afternoon.

"Our household was always full of song," Haza recalls. "My mother was a singer in Yemen, who would perform at henna pre-wedding ceremonies (see chapter 6). "On Saturday evenings neighbors would crowd onto our porch, and my mother would lead the singing...My six older sisters and two brothers would come home singing Elvis and the Beatles, and I would sing their tunes along with my mother's old Yemenite melodies."

Ofra Haza has brought the mixture of Eastern and Western music she absorbed at home to audiences in five continents. Called "one of the world's most accomplished singers" by London's *Melody Maker*, she was the grand prize winner at the 1989 Tokyo Music Festival. Her songs have hit the "Top 10" dance charts around the world.

A volunteer helps a newly-arrived Ethiopian immigrant family settle in.

The Ethiopians

The Ethiopian Jews have faced untold hardships on their journey to Israel. The first great wave of Ethiopian immigrants arrived in the winter of 1984–1985, in the covert "Operation Moses" airlift. Many had spent weeks walking through jungle and desert, facing danger, hunger, and thirst, to reach the planes that transported them to Israel. Not everyone survived. When the operation was abruptly stopped midway by premature publicity, many families were left divided. Children who had been sent to Israel ahead of their parents were left alone; husbands and wives were separated.

It was not until May 1991, when an emergency 26-hour airlift brought 14,000 Ethiopian Jews to Israel, that many of these families were reunited.

For the Ethiopian women, adjusting to a new life in Israel is a formidable challenge. Many have spent their lives in small, isolated mud-hut villages. Apartment buildings, electricity, supermarkets, and the Hebrew language represent only part of the transition they face. In Ethiopia, women's roles were clearly defined by tradition. Mothers taught their daughters to bake *injera*, the round, porous bread eaten with a spicy stew; to weave colorful baskets; and to make pottery. Girls married at about 16 and sometimes as young as 13. The families would arrange the marriage, usually with someone from a different village to make sure there was no blood relation. The young couple had little to say about the matter. The young brides, some leaving their families for the first time, would go to live in their husbands' villages. Women strictly observed the biblical laws of family purity by moving into a separate hut during menstruation.

Out of Africa The move to Israel disrupted the customs and functions that shaped the Ethiopian women's lives. At the hotels and immigrant hostels where they were initially housed, even the physical facilities were at first lacking—the separate women's houses, the round, flat pans for baking *injera*. The surrounding society moved at a different pace and followed different rules.

Many of the younger Ethiopian women have taken up the challenge of becoming part of this society. Some are attending universities and teachers' colleges; many are learning to be nurses, dressmakers, dental assistants, bookkeepers, and child care workers. Young Ethiopian women have already completed officers' training in the army.

Anyone who has met the Ethiopians has been deeply moved by their gentleness, their dignity, and their quiet patience in the face of the pain they have endured.

Traditions and transitions

Deborah Weissman, who teaches Israel's first comprehensive university-level course on women in Judaism, has entitled the course "Traditions and Transitions"—aptly describing the dilemmas of all Israeli women who face both the power of the old and the pull of the new within their communities.

Jewish religious life

The Jewish religious tradition is a strong and pervasive force in Israel, shaping many aspects of women's lives. In recent years, a growing number of Jewish women have begun to carve out active roles in the traditionally male domains of public prayer, study of the traditional texts, and religious leadership.

Women reading the Torah. Some women are taking more active roles in Jewish religious life.

BEING WOMAN 63

Nehama Leibowitz:

The dean of Israel's Bible teachers, Nehama Leibowitz is the inspiration and model for many of the younger women (and men) who are teaching Torah in Israel and elsewhere today. Born in Riga in 1905 and living in Jerusalem since 1926, Dr. Leibowitz—Nehama to her students and masses of admirers—is renowned worldwide for her scholarship and even more so for her skills and devotion as a master teacher.

In addition to her university students, Nehama has reached hundreds of thousands of others through weekly radio lessons and her study guides for the Bible portion read every Sabbath in the synagogue. Translated from Hebrew into several languages, these weekly self-instruction sheets have been distributed around the world. With characteristic modesty, she has paid tribute to the army of students who have communicated with her by mail, telephone and telegraph. In 1956, Nehama Leibowitz was awarded the Israel Prize for her work.

Many of these women are active in law, medicine, art, education, and a dozen other fields, these women believe that they need not remain passive spectators in religious life. Strongly committed to both Jewish tradition and women's equality, they believe that the two do not have to conflict but can enhance each other.

Study The past decade has seen an explosion of religious study for women. Women are learning the traditional Jewish sources which, with rare exceptions, have been taught to men only for centuries. In Jerusalem alone over a dozen schools are devoted to higher religious studies for women.

Some of the students are young women just before or just after college; others manage large families and full-time jobs and study at night after their children are asleep. For many, learning Torah, the Jewish religious tradition, is far more than an intellectual exercise: They work hard at cracking the ancient texts in search of their wisdom and insights, in the belief that the traditional sources can teach them how to live their daily lives.

Prayer For centuries, custom—but not necessarily religious law—has kept women from playing an active role in communal prayer. In the orthodox synagogue, women are separated from men by a curtain or partition and sometimes sit in a separate balcony or room. Some groups of women have begun holding their own services, but this is still rare in Israel.

In many non-orthodox synagogues—Reform, Conservative, and others—women play active and equal roles. While the non-orthodox movements are growing in number and influence, they still represent a minority and are not officially recognized in Israel.

The women's section of the Western Wall in Jerusalem.

The Women of the Wall

At seven o'clock on a chilly morning in December 1988, a group of 26 women walked to the Western Wall in Jerusalem, a site of powerful religious and historical symbolism for the Jews, and began to pray. The women brought a Torah scroll with them and some wore prayer shawls. While nothing the women did violated religious law, their reading from the scroll, wearing prayer shawls, and praying out loud in a group was seen by some as a radical break with tradition. Some of the ultra-Orthodox worshippers at the Wall responded with curses and physical attacks. Thus began a long controversy over the women's right to pray as they wished and over who controls the holy site.

Despite the violence, the Women of the Wall, as they came to be known, came back to pray at the Wall every Friday and on the first of every Hebrew month, traditionally a day of celebration for women. The prayers continue, with anywhere from 20 to 70 women participating. A temporary court order has forbidden the women from praying with prayer shawls and Torah scrolls and singing out loud. The group has petitioned Israel's High Court of Justice for the right to pray as they see fit and a legal decision is pending.

Spiritual Leader

When Gilah Dror applied for the job of rabbi of a congregation in Beersheba, in southern Israel, her being a woman was a major issue for the congregation. "They liked the kind of rabbinate I projected," says Gilah Dror, 41, "but they weren't sure they wanted a woman." Yet the congregation voted almost unanimously to hire her and is delighted with its new leader.

Gilah Dror, who practiced law for several years before studying for the rabbinate, is particularly enthusiastic about the service aspect of her position. She sees teaching and educating as important functions but only parts of her many-faceted job. She is involved in many other aspects of community life, such as conducting bar and bat mitzvah celebrations and helping the members of her congregation mark other major events in their lives. "It is a privilege to serve a community as a rabbi," she says

She believes that, while women rabbis are not a solution for every community, many are ready to work with women in this new capacity: "If Israelis are willing to accept women as government leaders and Knesset members, why not as spiritual leaders as well?"

***

Women rabbis The handful of women rabbis in Israel are true pioneers. Most were ordained by the Reform, Conservative, or Reconstructionist movements in the U.S., where women in small but growing numbers have been serving as rabbis for almost 20 years. The Israeli Reform movement has begun ordaining women rabbis; the Israeli Conservative movement, as of December 1991, is in the process of discussing the question. Is Israeli society ready to accept women rabbis? Some can see women in the rabbinical role of teacher, of religious educator, but are uncomfortable with women in other functions, such as leading prayers in the synagogue.

Ultra-Orthodox women

In the ultra-Orthodox world, tradition far outweighs transition. Living in separate communities in Jerusalem and other cities, Israel's estimated 270,000–300,000 ultra-Orthodox represent islands with their own rules and their own values. Their world is in some ways closer to Eastern Europe of a hundred years ago than Israel of today, in which every detail of life is governed by the strictest interpretation of Jewish religious law.

Far from monolithic, ultra-Orthodox society comprises numerous sub-groups and variations. Yet certain features are shared. One of these, as the visitor to Jerusalem's Mea She'arim or similar neighborhoods will immediately notice, is children in great numbers: three-year-olds wheeling younger siblings in their carriages, toddlers carrying infants, pregnant women with three or four lively preschoolers in tow. At least six children are the norm, 12 or more are not uncommon. In some neighborhoods, 40% of the population is under six.

Ultra-Orthodox Jews.

Most of these children grow up insulated from the secular world outside. There is no TV in their homes, and often no radio or secular books or newspapers. Their stories are from the Bible and Jewish history; many have never heard of Mickey Mouse or Donald Duck.

Modesty Also apparent is that even little girls wear long dresses, long sleeves, and tights. Married women cover their hair with wigs, scarves, or hats. Many women wear sedate shades of gray, black, or blue, no attention-getting reds. This concern with modesty often takes forms that seem extreme by Western standards. In some groups, boys and girls are forbidden to play together from about age 10. Pictures of women never appear in ultra-Orthodox newspapers. Some stores have separate hours for men and women customers; some men stand on buses rather than sit next to a woman. At weddings and other family celebrations, men and women sit separately and are often separated by a partition, if not a wall.

BEING WOMAN 67

Married life Women are usually married by age 20, many as young as 17. And once she is married, a woman begins to carry a serious burden. For the highest value in this society is religious study for men, and the women's supreme purpose is to enable their husbands to engage in such study, full-time if possible. For a great many ultra-Orthodox women, the combination of a large family and a student husband means that work outside the home and even outside the community is a necessity. The ideal job is teaching in an ultra-Orthodox school, or clerical or secretarial work within the community.

But the women seeking work now outnumber these jobs, and more and more are working outside the community in such fields as computers, graphics, book-keeping, nursing, or laboratory work. While women are now increasingly being trained in these areas, most men are taught religious studies only and do not even learn math or English after age 12. Their chances of finding employment in the secular world are thus quite poor. Thus while the men remain largely confined to the world of the *yeshiva* ("ye-SHI-va"), the religious studies academy, it is the women who, working in order to enable them to stay there, may be bringing the winds of change into a community that is doing its best to keep them out.

Helping hands How do these women manage their large families and jobs, with little assistance from husbands totally devoted to study and prayer? One answer lies in the tremendous women's support system in the ultra-Orthodox neighborhoods. Whether she is facing sick children, debts, or planning a wedding, a woman in this community is not alone. Women watch each other's children, pool resources, and sometimes pay each other's bills. When a woman gives birth, neighbors bring in hot meals to her family for a week. A North American observer noted that it is almost like living in a commune.

The second and perhaps most important answer is the women's belief, inculcated from earliest childhood, that they are fulfilling a divinely-ordained function by living as they do. This gives them much inner strength and the serenity to deal with circumstances, such as eight children in a two-and-a-half room apartment, that would leave most women anything but serene.

The ultra-Orthodox women are supported by the total confidence that they are giving their children the best of all possible values. Says a mother of 12, "Our children's lives are so clearly defined for them; they see things with such clarity. While we encourage our children to think, they seem so happy, so content, so satisfied. If they have any questions, they have answers too."

A group of Arab women gather at the Damascus Gate market in Jerusalem.

Arab women

Arab women face formidable dilemmas of tradition and transition. Starting in the early 1950s, when Arab girls began to attend school in large numbers, Arab women have been creating new roles in a society where tradition is a powerful force.

Values governing male–female relations represent the strongest traditional force for Arab women. For while growing numbers are breaking new ground in study and work, the concept of "family honor" is still held sacred in many towns and villages. Family honor refers to what is considered proper behavior for a woman: no physical intimacy before marriage, and according to the stricter interpretations, no social contact or even casual conversation between men and women.

Women who violate this code are seen as destroying the honor of their entire family, with sometimes disastrous results. In one of the most painful problems for Arab society, women are still killed by their own relatives for "dishonoring" their families or being suspected of doing so. In the absence of statistics, estimates range from four to 40 such killings a year. But they are on the decline, partly due to the efforts of Arab women's groups who have broken traditional taboos and publicly protested the "family honor" killings.

Between two worlds In many villages, the birth of a son is still greeted with far more joy than the birth of a daughter, and girls are taught from earliest childhood that their only role is to be a wife and mother and to be subservient to men. At the same time, the number of Arab women studying at Israeli universities has snowballed. These women face a complex set of dilemmas.

For example, finding the right partner is not a simple matter for independent and educated Arab women. While there are indications that a growing number of Arab men look for wives who are educated and who can help support the family, many still want their wives to fulfill the traditional roles. An Arab woman attending Haifa University says that even men who study abroad "come back to the village and marry high school girls whom they can tell what to do, who will stay home and wash the dishes."

> "During the wars, we, as mothers, suffer twice as much—first for our own flesh and blood, and again for our Jewish neighbors and friends with whom we share our everyday lives. The Palestinian problem is painful for us. We are anxious for peace, a lasting peace which secures safety and dignity for both sides."
> — *Khitam Massarwa, wife of Israel's first Arab consul general*

University study also moves women toward political involvement, a new experience for many of them. "You have to join a party on campus," says Nadya, an education student at the Hebrew University in Jerusalem. "Students who are apathetic are put under a lot of pressure to show very quickly where they stand." She contrasts this with her home town of Nazareth, where "society doesn't accept women being politically involved."

When Arab women received the vote along with all other citizens in 1948 (becoming the first women in the Middle East to win suffrage), they did not necessarily gain a political voice. For many years, they simply voted along with their husbands or the head of the clan—thus doubling the clan's political power. This is no longer the case, and younger women especially are making their own choices in the voting booth.

A minority within a minority All this is further complicated by Arab women's position as a minority within a minority, torn by what they see as a conflict between their people (the Palestinians) and their state (Israel). Israeli laws—in particular the compulsory education law and those banning polygamy, divorce without consent, and child marriage—have made a vast difference in the lives of Arab women. At the same time, many identify with the Palestinian uprising in the West Bank and Gaza.

The Islamic movement Recent years have seen an upsurge of the Islamic movement, advocating a return to strict Moslem piety. In towns and villages where the movement is strong, high school girls no longer wear jeans but rather floor-length gowns with long sleeves and head cowls. Boys and girls sit in separate classes, rather than studying together as they do in most towns. Yet traditional dress does not always mean traditional behavior. While some of the Islamic movement women believe their only role should be caring for home and children, others are social and political activists. "They are encouraged to attend university and to drive their own cars," says Haifa educator Maryam Mar'i. "And when there is a call for voters, it includes both men and women voters."

An Arab student at the Hebrew University in Jerusalem. Compulsory elementary education has opened the doors of higher learning to women in the Arab community.

> The number of Arab women studying at Israeli universities doubled between 1969 and 1972, doubled between 1977 and 1981, and doubled again by 1985, with nearly 1,200 Arab women on campuses.

BEING WOMAN 71

Working within tradition Perhaps the most successful advocates of change for Arab women are those who have found ways of working within tradition rather than against it. This approach is exemplified by Nelly Karkabi, a Christian Arab who heads the Arab Women's Department of Na'amat, the women's labor organization.

She cites a lesson she learned very early in the game, in the 1950s, when her major efforts were directed toward convincing men to allow their wives and daughters to work. She and her colleagues at Na'amat organized tours of the factories that offered jobs. They showed families where the women would work and where they would eat, pointed out that the supervisors were female, and explained how the women would travel to and from their jobs. She arranged special transportation, financed by the factories, because parents would not allow their daughters to stand alone at a bus stop or travel with strange men. "the main lesson I learned in those days has remained with me until now," she says, "great respects for tradition, for without its blessing we have no chance of bringing progress to the Arab women."

It was once said that there is no need to name an Arab girl because her entire identity is determined by the men in her life: first she is known as "daughter of," then as "wife of," and finally as "mother of." While in some villages this is still the case, the changes within one

Violet Khoury

Some women have enough ability, courage, and stature to create new roles and pave the way for others. One of these was Violet Khoury. Descended from 14 generations of Greek Orthodox priests, Khoury was a pioneer in many areas. Her unconventional path began in 1949 when she became the first Arab woman in Israel to study social work. Her work took her traveling alone among the villages of the Galilee, not quite acceptable for a proper young woman, and she did not marry until the relatively advanced age of 24. Her marriage was arranged, to a man 18 years her senior. Some 30 years later, she said: "It wasn't a marriage of love—and I have no regrets. In a marriage of love, I wouldn't have received the trust and freedom my husband gave me—even though he sometimes complained that his shirts weren't ironed or his dinner was late, and that I was taking care of the whole world, but not my sons."

In 1969, Violet Khoury succeeded her husband as a member of the local council of her town, Kafr Yassif. In 1972, she was elected mayor—another first for an Arab woman. In December 1987, Violet Khoury died of cancer at the age of 58, leaving a legacy of expanded opportunities for all Arab women.

generation—a moment in historical terms—have been vast. Says Khitam Massarwa: "We are still only at the beginning of a long road on which we must proceed with patience and common sense. If we can improve women's status and at the same time keep the closeness of our families, then we can say we have truly made progress."

Druze women

Living in 18 mountain villages in northern Israel, the country's 80,000 Druze constitute a distinct national and religious group within the Arab community. When the Druze broke away from Islam in the 11th century, among the points of difference were issues of women's status: Unlike Islam, the Druze religion allows men to marry only one wife, forbids girls from marrying before age 15, supports women's right to choose their own husbands, and gives daughters equal inheritance rights with sons.

At the same time, the strongly traditional Druze society has kept women largely confined to their homes and villages for hundreds of years. For this tightly-knit community (the Druze religion is secret and intermarriage is forbidden) change has come only during recent decades.

For the Druze woman, as for other women in the Arab community, Israel's compulsory education law has been a major force for change. Most girls now complete not only elementary school but also a vocational or academic secondary school. An increasing number are going on to teachers' colleges or other higher education. Many of the younger Druze women choose smaller families and are raising three or four children rather than six to ten as did their mothers.

A Druze woman out in the countryside with her family.

BEING WOMAN 73

The first Druze schoolgirl

The youngest of six daughters of an important Druze sheikh in the village of Dalyat el-Carmel, Huriya Birani was seven when the State of Israel was established in 1948. Until then, the community schools had been open only to boys. Taking advantage of the new state's compulsory education law, Huriya's father defied Druze custom and enrolled her in the local school. Huriya graduated from eighth grade as the only girl in a class of 49 boys, becoming the first Druze girl in Israel to complete elementary school.

There were no high schools in the village at the time, and even Huriya's unconventional father could not allow her to commute to a Jewish school in nearby Haifa, as some of the boys did. But he did encourage her to converse with the many Israeli and foreign visitors who frequented their home, rather than play the traditional women's role of serving food and then disappearing. Huriya mastered Hebrew and English and learned about the world beyond Dalyat.

For Huriya's own six children, things are quite different. There is now a high school in Dalyat el-Carmel. And in contrast to the days when Huriya was a teenager, today girls in the village commute to Haifa for studies. One of Huriya's daughters is studying at Haifa University to become a teacher of Hebrew literature. A number of women in Dalyat work as teachers, medical secretaries, or bank clerks. More women would like to work, says Huriya, but finding a job is a problem, for custom still prevents many Druze women from working outside their villages.

For Huriya and for other pacesetters in the community, the commitment to the Druze religion and tradition—symbolized by the married woman's white headscarf—is still strong. They have expanded their horizons immeasurably while remaining—physically and in many ways spiritually—within the villages of their ancestors.

Christian women

There have been Christian communities in the land since the times of Jesus. They represent a minority group within the largely Moslem Arab community.

In addition, some 8,000 priests, nuns, and teachers associated with various Christian orders from around the world work in schools, hospitals, monasteries, and convents throughout the country.

Traditionally well-educated, Christian women became the first teachers when Arab girls began attending school in growing numbers after 1948. The Christian schools are regarded as among Israel's finest. Many of the nuns living in Israel devote their lives to extremely important work in caring for orphans, the retarded, the handicapped, the elderly and the terminally ill of all religions.

Nuns on the Via Dolorosa in Jerusalem. Putting their Christian faith into practice, nuns work in many spheres of community service—caring for the elderly or the disabled, or running schools and orphanages.

Sister Itha

Sister Itha of the St. Charles Hospice in Jerusalem describes herself with a smile as a *sabra* ("SAHB-ra")—the popular term for a native Israeli who, like the *sabra* cactus, is said to be prickly on the outside but sweet on the inside. Though not prickly, Sister Itha says that after 55 years in Jerusalem she is more at home there than in her native Germany.

The Jerusalem hospice was founded in 1893 as part of the charitable order of St. Charles of Borromeo. At various times in its history, the hospice has operated schools, clinics, and old age homes. Today the 18 German, Rumanian, and Israeli Arab nuns at St. Charles conduct a kindergarten and elementary school for Christian Arab children and a hospice for pilgrims and visitors of all religions and nationalities. "Here we are all one family," says Sister Itha.

Now an island of serenity on a quiet Jerusalem street, the St. Charles Hospice has seen less peaceful times. Sister Itha remembers the 1948 War of Independence, when Jerusalem was cut off from the rest of the country and food and water were strictly rationed. "Since we were the only ones with a big cistern, we shared the water with all our neighbors," she recalls. "We had a supply of flour, so we baked bread and our neighbors came to get bread for their children." When she speaks of her hopes and prayers for peace in the Holy Land and in the world, Sister Itha's eyes fill with tears. "I have seen too many wars," she says. "When will it stop? We constantly pray that war and violence will end. As long as we pray, God will protect us."

BEING WOMAN

War and peace

Since its birth, Israel has been engaged in a complex and painful conflict with its Palestinian and other Arab neighbors. This tragic struggle has caused untold suffering on all sides and deeply affects the life of every Israeli woman.

Jewish, Druze, and many Bedouin men serve in the army from ages 18 to 21 and most are called up for reserve duty for a month or two a year until age 51. Every woman in these communities is the friend, daughter, sister, wife, or mother of a soldier; anxiety, casualties, and bereavement are part of life. The men's intense involvement in defense moves many women to an equally intense absorption in feeding and caring for the soldiers in their families, especially in times of war or tension. During the 1973 Yom Kippur War, when many men were mobilized for up to six months, women baked so many cakes that they caused a flour shortage.

An Arab and a Jewish boy. Mothers in both communities share the yearning that their children will grow up in peace.

Since the outbreak of the *intifada* (Palestinian uprising in the West Bank and Gaza Strip) in December 1987, a growing number of women have taken a stand on the conflict and found ways to make their voices heard. Women's protest movements range from the Women in Black, who stage weekly silent vigils condemning the Israeli occupation of the West Bank and Gaza, to the Women in White, who oppose territorial compromise. Women's efforts have often focused on the human pain and suffering caused by the conflict and urged negotiation rather than force.

United by the dream of their children growing up in peace, small groups of Arab and Jewish women are working toward dialogue and mutual understanding. Poet and author Dr. Ada Aharoni helped found The Bridge, a woman-to-woman organization devoted to coexistence. "Women in both Jewish and Arab society are brought up to be the family peacemakers," says Aharoni. The Egyptian-born Aharoni, president of the International Congress of Poets, was recently awarded the "International Peace Poem" prize by UNESCO's International Academy for Arts and Culture for her book *Goodbye to Wars*.

Women in the military

Israel is one of very few countries to draft women into compulsory military service and was the first to recruit women by national law. All Jewish 18-

year-olds are candidates for service in the Israel Defense Forces (IDF) when they finish high school. Compulsory service is 24 months for women, and some volunteer for more. In practice, some 65% of the 18-year-old women actually serve in the army. Married women and mothers are exempt (but may volunteer), as are women who declare that their religious beliefs prevent them from serving. (Many of these perform alternative national service in schools, hospitals, children's institutions, or elsewhere.) Some women are disqualified on medical or other grounds.

Women are eligible for reserve duty until age 24 or until their marriage or the birth of their first child. Dentists, physicians, physiotherapists, occupational therapists, and surgical nurses often serve in the reserves for several more years.

> *A Bridge of Peace*
> My dear Arab sister
> Let us build
> A sturdy bridge
> From your world to mine
> And from mine to yours
> over the vast ridge of prejudice
> And hold hands high
> Full of stars of twinkling peace
> Above men's heads
> To the open sky.
> —Ada Aharoni

During the past 10 to 15 years, a great many new military jobs have opened up for women. While in the past a large proportion were relegated to clerical or secretarial work, today young women of 18, 19, and 20 bear serious responsibility in many branches of the military. The number of women officers has tripled in the past ten years. In theory and increasingly in practice, any job that does not involve combat is open to women.

The Women in Black demonstrate against the Israeli occupation of the West Bank and Gaza.

BEING WOMAN 77

Living in a land torn by war, a mother mourns her soldier-son.

More jobs for women The Israeli army does a great deal of educational work, with both new immigrant soldiers and veteran Israelis in need of remedial education. Almost all of this teaching is done by women. Women do highly classified intelligence work. While women do not engage in combat they do train men in combat units. Women train men to operate tanks and teach mine detection. Almost all the instructors in the Artillery Corps are women. Serving as operations officers, women plan military operations and explain them to soldiers. Among the other jobs open to women are auto and aircraft mechanics, bomb disposal, cartography, electronics, weather forecasting, and decoding air photography. Women serve as air force flight controllers, command navy tug-boats, and fly as radar operators on naval reconnaissance aircraft.

Says Brigadier General Hedva Almog, former commander of the Women's Corps: "Were we to take all the women out of the IDF for a day, it simply wouldn't function."

Amira Dotan

When Amira Dotan became the first Israeli woman to reach the rank of Brigadier General in 1988, she was hailed as the first Jewish woman general since the biblical Deborah waged war against the Canaanites 3,000 years ago. During her five years as commander of the Women's Corps, Dotan did a great deal to open new military jobs for women. While she believes that women are physically and psychologically capable of serving as combat soldiers, this is not a function she advocates. Sending women into battle, she believes, would violate essential Jewish values. "We cannot ignore our heritage. There is a special role for the Jewish woman as mother and center of the family. I fight for equal opportunities for male and female soldiers but we must recognize that there are certain differences."

As commander of the Women's Corps, Dotan sought to encourage young women to take on the more challenging military jobs, especially those involving technology. She organized a program in which women soldiers in non-traditional jobs visited high schools to serve as role models for girls about to begin their army service. An impressive model herself, Dotan was raising three children and completing an M.A. in psychology when she became commander of the Women's Corps at age 35. While recognizing the potential conflicts between family and career, she advises young women that the combination "is your right and you can do it." (Picture shows Amira Dotan during target practice.)

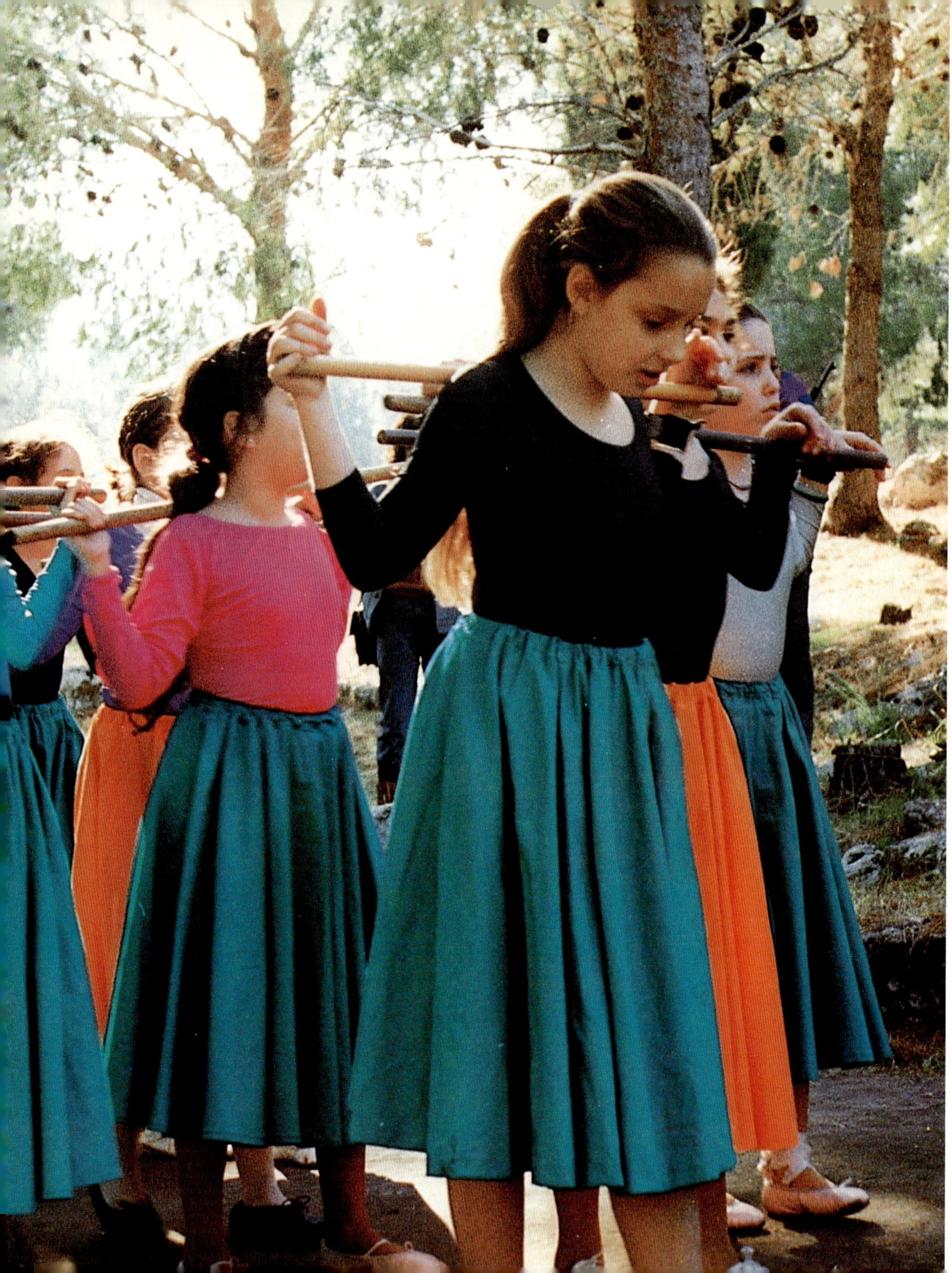

chapter five

Profiles of Women

T he lives of these six women span the past 100 years—a time of conflict and challenge, and a time when dreams became reality. The task of creating a new society in a new country inspired many to place the common good above their own private needs, comfort, and safety. Each of these six women has responded to that call in her own way and each has given her people something unique.

For each of these women, what has been important was not to receive from society, but to contribute, to lead and to inspire. Each has changed the world she found—and each represents many thousands of lesser-known women who have contributed on a smaller scale but with equal devotion.

Hannah Senesh

In August 1936, Hannah Senesh wrote in her diary: "I would rather be an unusual person than just average…I would like to be a great soul, if God will permit!" The next day, she added: "Big soul! I am so far from anything like that. I'm just a struggling 15-year-old whose principal preoccupation is coping with herself."

Hannah could not have imagined then how one day she would indeed become a "great soul" and serve as an inspiration for her people.

Opposite: Schoolgirls in an outdoor performance. These schoolgirls and others like them will have many challenging roles to perform when they grow up and become the next generation of women in Israeli society.

Right: Hannah Senesh with her brother.

PROFILES OF WOMEN 81

"Something to believe in" Born in Budapest, Hungary, in 1921, Hannah's first dream was to be a writer, like her father who had died when she was six. In the diary she started keeping when she was 13, she wrote: "At first I decided I would write only about beautiful and serious things, and not constantly about boys, as most girls do. But it looks as if it's not possible to exclude boys from the life of a 15-year-old girl." Along with her "beautiful and serious" thoughts, Hannah's diary tells of tennis, swimming, and ping-pong; of her new blue taffeta dress; of parties that lasted until dawn—and of a whole parade of boys.

When Hannah was 16, things began to change. Hitler's influence was spreading through Europe; Hungary passed laws barring Jews from being judges, teachers, or lawyers. Hannah was elected as an officer of her school's literary society but was prevented from holding the position because she was a Jew. Hannah's thoughts turned more and more toward Palestine, the historic Jewish homeland where pioneers were creating a new society. Her studies, parties, her graduation from high school lost much of their interest for her. "One needs something to believe in…to feel that one's life has meaning, that one is needed in this world," she wrote.

A special mission In 1939, soon after her 18th birthday, Hannah left her family and friends in Budapest and set off alone for a girls' agricultural training school in Palestine. World War II had just erupted.

Hannah was excited about being a pioneering farm worker in Palestine and wrote enthusiastic letters about washing cows and feeding chickens. But she sometimes felt frustrated by the drudgery despite her idealism and love for the land. One day, she wrote, was spent washing 150 pairs of socks.

And there was terrible news of the war in Europe. "The sky is a brilliant blue, peace and fertility fill the land," Hannah wrote in June 1940. "I would like to shout into the radio, 'It isn't true! It's a lie! It's a fraud that there are a million dead and countless injured, bombings, cities destroyed!' "

Hannah worried constantly about her mother in Budapest and dreamed of finding a way to rescue her—how, she

> "Day after tomorrow I am starting something new. Perhaps it's madness. Perhaps it's fantastic. Perhaps one in a hundred—or one in a thousand—pays with his life. Perhaps with less than his life, perhaps with more. Don't ask questions. You'll eventually know what it's about."
> *from Hannah's letter to her brother George, December 25, 1943, before she started paratroop training*

PROFILES OF WOMEN

was not sure. She began to feel that she would be entrusted with a special mission whose nature she did not yet know.

Two years later, Hannah learned that the British army was seeking volunteers to parachute into Nazi-occupied Europe to rescue downed airmen and help organize resistance. She immediately seized the opportunity and volunteered for the dangerous job.

"Blessed is the match" On March 13, 1944, Hannah and several comrades parachuted into Yugoslavia, near the Hungarian border. A comrade later wrote that Hannah, the only woman who had ever parachuted into Yugoslavia from a friendly country, "knew how to talk to a general as well as a private" and was unmistakably the leader of the group. Hannah and her comrades walked hundreds of miles through snow, swam icy rivers, and fought in the forests along with the Yugoslavian partisans.

When Hannah parted from her friends before crossing into Nazi-occupied Hungary, she gave one of them a scrap of paper which he almost threw away. It was the poem "Blessed is the Match," which today many Israelis know by heart.

Soon after crossing the border, Hannah was captured and imprisoned in her native Budapest. She was tortured by the Nazis and beaten so severely that four of her teeth were broken, but she revealed nothing. Her courage won the respect of even her jailers, who said she was stronger than 10 men. In November 1944, just weeks before the Soviets liberated Budapest, Hannah was executed by firing squad. She was 23.

Blessed is the Match
Blessed is the match that is burnt
    while kindling flames.
Blessed is the flame that burns
    secretly in the heart.
Blessed is the heart with the strength
    to stop beating with honor.
Blessed is the match that is burnt
    while kindling flames.

Yugoslavia, May 1944

Budapest prison cell.

The courage and spirit of Hannah Senesh have become part of Israeli folklore. Every schoolchild learns her poems; some of them have been set to music and become popular songs. Thirty-two streets in Israeli towns and cities bear her name.

Hannah once wrote: "There are stars whose radiance is visible on earth though they have long been extinct. There are people whose brilliance continues to light the world though they are no longer among the living. These lights are particularly bright when the night is dark." For her people, Hannah Senesh became such a light.

Above: Hannah Senesh

Right: The life and writing of Hannah Senesh shine like bright stars in a dark night.

A bright star Hannah Senesh was at once introspective and vulnerable, strong, daring, and determined. It is this combination that has captured the imagination of her people and made her a national legend: Hannah the paratrooper with a pistol on her belt, Hannah the poet, and Hannah the loving young woman who made paper dolls for the children sharing her

84   PROFILES OF WOMEN

Golda Meir

Golda Meir's earliest memories are of cold, hunger, and fear. The woman who became Israel's fourth prime minister was born in 1898 to a poor Jewish family in Kiev. "I was always a little too cold outside and a little too empty inside," she wrote in her autobiography. She remembers her father barricading the house against angry mobs looking for Jews and her anger that all her father could do to protect her was to nail a few planks to the door. "Above all I remember being aware that this was happening to me because I was Jewish, which made me different from most of the other children in the yard," she wrote. Golda was left with "the profound instinctive belief that if one wanted to survive, one had to take effective action about it personally."

When Golda was eight, her family, like many other East European Jews, left Russia in search of a better life in the United States.

Milwaukee

As new immigrants in Milwaukee, Wisconsin, the family was still poor, and Golda was often late for school because she had to help tend her mother's grocery store. But Golda enjoyed her Milwaukee years and especially her school. When she was 71 and Israel's prime minister, she went back to visit the Fourth Street elementary school and met with the pupils there—children of hard-working minorities as she had been.

When she graduated from eighth grade, Golda knew exactly what she wanted to do—go on to high school and eventually become a teacher. But her parents had other plans for her: She would work in the grocery, maybe go to secretarial school, and marry a family friend named Mr. Goodstein. Golda was not about to go along with this program. When her sister Sheyna and her husband invited her to live with them in Denver, Golda, then 15, seized the chance. One night, she lowered a bundle of clothes to a friend waiting in the street, left a note for her parents, and the next morning took the train to Denver.

Golda Meir

PROFILES OF WOMEN 85

Denver Sheyna's house in Denver was a gathering place for young Jewish immigrants from Russia. They would stay up far into the night, drinking endless cups of tea with lemon and talking about everything under the sun, and especially the young socialist pioneers in Palestine. The idea of building a new egalitarian society where Jews could be independent captured Golda's imagination, and she dreamed of joining the pioneers. It was also at her sister's home in Denver that Golda met Morris Meyerson, the gentle and intelligent young man she married a few years later, when she was almost 20.

Golda soon became active in the Zionist socialist movement, traveling around the country making speeches and raising funds. Soon after World War I, Golda and Morris left the security of the U.S. for the precarious life of a pioneer in Palestine.

> "I took a great deal with me from America to Palestine, more perhaps than I can express—an understanding of the meaning of freedom, an awareness of the opportunities offered to the individual in a true democracy, and a permanent nostalgia for the great beauty of the American countryside."
>
> — *Golda Meir*

Palestine Golda and Morris joined Kibbutz Merhavia, a young communal settlement in the Jezreel Valley. Life on a kibbutz in the 1920s meant exhausting labor and very little to eat. Yet Golda found much to like in kibbutz life, especially the rewards of taking part in a great social experiment and creating a new collective society. True to her nature, she soon became active in setting kibbutz policy. But Morris, a quiet and reserved person who loved books and music, was unsuited to communal life and hard physical work. He became ill and they had to leave the kibbutz. Golda quickly rose to leadership in the socialist labor movement in Palestine and held a series of key positions in the Histadrut, the powerful general labor federation.

During the early years of her public career, Golda struggled with the often conflicting demands of her work and of mothering her two young children. It was also during those years that the differences between Golda and Morris led to their separation. "I had to be what I was, and what I was made it impossible for him to have the sort of wife he wanted and needed," she wrote.

On November 29, 1947, the United Nations voted to partition Palestine into an Arab and Jewish state. It was then clear that the State of Israel would come into being—and equally clear that the new state would not survive its birth without arms to defend itself against the

The embassy in Moscow

Golda Meir decided that the representatives of Israel, a young, poor, struggling country, should "face the world without makeup"—no lavish entertainment or conspicuous consumption of any kind. Her embassy was run like a kibbutz, with everyone working together, eating together, and getting the same amount of pocket money. Instead of eating in the dining room of their hotel, Golda and her staff bought cheese, bread, and eggs at an outdoor market and prepared meals in their rooms.

When Golda and the embassy staff went to the Moscow Great Synagogue on Rosh Hashana, the Jewish new year, they were surrounded by thousands of Jews who—against clear warnings by the Soviet authorities—came to show their identification with the new state of Israel. Golda felt that she was "caught up in a torrent of love so strong that it literally took my breath away and slowed down my heart." The photograph of Golda surrounded by the Moscow Jews appears on Israel's 10-shekel bill—popularly known as "a Golda."

---

imminent attack from its neighbors. Early in 1948—so urgently that she took only a coat with her—Golda was sent to the U.S. to raise funds to purchase those arms.

In another important mission, Golda met secretly with King Abdallah of Transjordan (grandfather of the present Jordanian King Hussein) to try to dissuade him from joining Egypt, Syria, Lebanon, and Iraq in attacking Israel. Disguised in the robes and veil of a Moslem woman, she made a dangerous trip to the king in Amman just days before the state was proclaimed. (King Abdallah, probably against his will, did in fact join the attack on Israel.)

Golda signed Israel's Declaration of Independence (May 14, 1948), the only American Jew among the signatories, and was soon appointed the new state's ambassador to the Soviet Union.

Cabinet Minister Golda next served as Minister of Labor (1949–1956), and recalled her seven years in that job as the most satisfying of her life. She initiated programs to create housing and jobs for the thousands of new immigrants pouring into the country.

In 1956, Golda was appointed Israel's second foreign minister, then the only woman in the world to hold such a position. Particularly close to her heart was the International Cooperation Program, in which Israel shared its expertise in agriculture and other areas with emerging nations, especially in Africa. As a citizen of a young country, she felt a special kinship with the people of the new African countries. "We shared with the Africans not only the challenge posed by the need for rapid development, but also the memory of centuries of suffering," she said.

> On one of her many visits to Africa, Golda was made a paramount chief of the Gola tribe of northern Liberia—an honor rarely bestowed on women. "I was dressed in the bright robes of a paramount chief and underwent a secret initiation, the details of which I have no intention of disclosing. What I can say about the ceremony is that I was immensely impressed and delighted by the colorfulness, the naturalness, and the wholeheartedness of the proceedings. They had the kind of warmth and joy about them that made me feel immediately at home wherever I went in Africa."

Prime minister In 1969, Golda was called out of retirement to replace Prime Minister Levi Eshkol, who died suddenly in office. It was not a job she sought. "I could certainly understand the reservations of those…who thought that a 70-year-old grandmother was hardly the perfect candidate to head a 20-year-old state," she later wrote.

As prime minister, Golda had to make some of the most painful decisions of her life. The Yom Kippur War of October 1973, when Israel was caught unprepared by a surprise Syrian and Egyptian attack, was a time of great agony for the country and for Golda as prime minister.

In retrospect, Golda knew that had she made an earlier decision to call up the reserves—against the advice of her military and intelligence experts—she could have saved the lives of many young men. "I will never again be the person I was before the Yom Kippur War," she later said. Yet many saw her calm and steadfast leadership during the war as her finest hour.

In June 1974, after 50 years of public service, after having been hailed as one of the most admired women in the world, Golda Meir retired. Golda's biographer Ralph Martin said that she "lived in a state of emergency, paid her dues, earned her greatness." She died in 1979, mourned as an outstanding leader who was always known to her people simply as "Golda."

Shoshana Damari

For Israelis, it is hard to imagine Israeli song—or Israel's history—without Shoshana Damari.

Universally acknowledged as the queen of Israeli song, she has sung for every important event in the country's history, from the pre-state days and the 1948 War of Independence to a special concert to mark the signing of the 1979 peace treaty with Egypt.

Much more than an entertainer, she became a national symbol before there was a nation. For half a century, she has sung for the troops in every war, her stage often two tanks hastily covered with nets and her backdrop the desert.

A powerful performer with a dramatic stage presence and a deep, throaty voice, Shoshana has sung in 15 languages and on every continent. She has appeared frequently at Carnegie Hall and Lincoln Center in New York and elsewhere throughout the U.S.

Yemenite song

Shoshana Damari carries on a long tradition of Yemenite women singers. For the Yemenite Jews, singing was always important, one of the few recreations allowed by the oppressive regime under which they lived. The Yemenites became well known for their fine voices and well-developed musical tradition.

Yemenite women created and embellished songs while working at handicrafts or celebrating family occasions. Possessing few books, they developed a rich oral tradition. Women knew prayers and long passages from the Bible by heart. They would sing prayers at home while men went to the synagogue. Women also composed their own songs, using poetry and song to comment on the events of the day.

Shoshana first sang with her mother, who sang traditional songs at weddings and special laments at mourning periods. As a girl, Shoshana would go with her. "When someone died, my mother would make up lyrics describing the person's personality and deeds. Of course, she would do it only for the people she knew. And when I went with my mother to sing at weddings, sometimes we would be there all night. We'd sing just two or three songs, but they lasted for hours."

She recalls those early years as her best school. "I loved singing and I loved my mother. If I hear a Yemenite prayer now, I remember my house on a Friday night with everyone singing around the table. Today I miss those traditions very much. With all the luxury I have and the admiration of audiences, there are certainly days when I miss the pleasure that I derived from those days singing the Yemenite music with my family."

Opposite: Golda Meir helped develop ties between Israel and African countries.

PROFILES OF WOMEN

Early years Shoshana Damari was brought to Israel from Yemen as a baby in 1922. "My mother used to tell me how they trekked across the desert with a few belongings, and donkeys to carry the children and water," she says. "When I became ill, the others told my mother to leave me behind as she still had four other children. But she gathered herbs to make a drug and somehow I got better."

At 13, Shoshana left home to study singing and acting at a Tel Aviv drama school. "Even today that would cause a sensation, so much more in those days. But my father was very understanding and refused to listen to the elders of the community, who said I would come under bad influences. Two years later, when I sang on the radio, they came to my father and shook his hand and told him I had brought pride to the Yemenite community." Shoshana made her first solo appearance at 17. By that time she was already married to Shlomo Bosmi, the director of her school, who was also her manager until he died in 1986. "He taught me everything," says Shoshana. "How to dress, how to move on stage, how to behave. He wouldn't let me eat ice cream in the street. He used to say, 'You are a queen, and queens don't lick ice cream cones in the street.'"

A style that lasts Shoshana has maintained her own distinctive performing style through changes of fashion, resisting suggestions to wear slinkier dresses or sing more provocative songs. "I am often asked by young singers why I never change my style to something lighter, more catchy and popular," says Shoshana. "I explain to them that mine are eternal songs, with texts and music which have made a lasting impression on the development of Hebrew song."

"My old songs were born with the state, and each has a special significance: 'Poppies' is about generations changing but flowers remaining the same—it makes people cry, recalls old memories. 'The Last Battle' was the song I sang to the first division that went out to fight in the War of Independence. Later I heard that most of them never returned. When people hear my songs, they each connect them with their own experiences."

Shoshana's father, a teacher, never let poverty keep him from singing. "One day he was sitting in front of his house in Yemen and singing while 'playing' a tin can," she says. Someone asked him why he was singing, what was the happy occasion. He said, "I have no bread and no money, but I don't sit and count what I don't have. My head is clear and I can sing."

Traditional Yemenite music has always been an important part of Shoshana's repertoire. "I'm a Yemenite and started my career with Yemenite songs. They are the love of my life," she says.

Putting traditional songs on stage requires some adaptation. "Sometimes I would sing traditional songs in concert and Yemenites would come to me and ask why I didn't finish the song. But you can't stand on stage and sing all 10 verses of a wedding song. Shortening it makes it more dramatic and interesting and more appropriate for a concert. Traditional songs are like raw diamonds. They shine when they are cut and polished." Shoshana believes that people are returning to traditional ethnic songs today not only out of nostalgia, but because they are simply beautiful.

"Homeward" Of her countless performances over the past 50 years, Damari especially remembers singing for refugees in Cyprus waiting to travel to Israel in 1947. "I stood and sang on a table, accompanied by a battered old piano. Perhaps the most moving song I sang that evening was 'Homeward,' which had a greater significance on that day than on any other before or since. At the end of the evening, a father with a small child pushed his way to the front of the crowd and his little girl presented me with a bouquet of carefully arranged dried weeds—it was more beautiful for me than any of the extravagant flower arrangements I have ever received after a show. Over the years many people have told me that the first time they heard me was in Cyprus."

For her contributions to Israel's song and spirit, Shoshana Damari was awarded the Israel Prize, the country's highest award, in 1987.

Shoshana Damari

Ida Nudel

When she arrived in Israel on October 15, 1987, Ida Nudel was already known throughout the world for her heroic struggle on behalf of the "refuseniks"—those who like herself were refused permission to leave the Soviet Union. Among the thousands waiting for her at the Tel Aviv airport that night was actress Jane Fonda, who had worked on her behalf. Fonda said, "I want to thank Ida Nudel for teaching me one very important thing: never lose hope, never lose hope."

A 16-year struggle As a university student in the 1950s, Ida Nudel was deeply affected by the 1953 "doctors' plot"—Stalin's trumped-up charge that Jewish doctors in the Kremlin had murdered important Russian officers (he had the doctors beaten incessantly until they "confessed"). Ida's response to Stalin's violent anti-Semitic campaign was not to hide her Jewish identity but to strengthen it. She began studying Hebrew, Jewish history, and the Jewish religion. She and her younger sister Elena closely followed what was happening in Israel. By 1971 they decided that they wanted to make Israel their home.

In May 1971, Ida, then 40, and Elena applied for permission to leave the Soviet Union. Elena and her husband and son were given permission and settled in Israel. Ida, an economist, was refused. Thus began a 16-year struggle.

Her request for an exit visa was first denied on the ground that she held "state secrets." (She in fact worked as an economist-engineer checking hygienic standards in food stores.) The authorities had her fired from her job and blacklisted in her profession. Ida continued her appeals and began writing letters of protest. She became the only woman visibly working in the emigration struggle.

She began to campaign for all refuseniks—telling their stories to tourists and international leaders, taking part in demonstrations and hunger strikes. The KGB harassed her, seizing her on the street and searching her, raiding her Moscow apartment, disconnecting her telephone, and confiscating her books, letters, and photographs. In 1973 Ida was imprisoned for 15 days for petitioning then General Secretary Leonid

> "We were like twins, but Ida was much stronger, more decisive. When our father was killed in the Battle of Stalingrad, Ida became the head of the family. She did carpentry. She was physically strong. When she took up ice skating, she became the champion of her university in Moscow. She was the best at diving. At her economic institute, she did what men couldn't do."
>
> — Elena Fridman, Ida Nudel's sister

Brezhnev to let her go. In 1977, Ida and 11 other refusenik women formed the Moscow Women's Liberation Group. They hoped that as women they would be less subject to arrests and harassments than men, but this was not the case.

In 1978, at a large demonstration of refusenik women and children, Ida hung a large banner from her window saying: "KGB, GIVE ME MY VISA!" For this, she was arrested and charged with the crime of "malicious hooliganism," brought to a closed trial, and convicted of "anti-Soviet activity." At her trial, Ida said that she looked back on the preceding period as "the most glorious years of my life. During those seven years I learned to walk proudly with my head high as a human being and as a Jewish woman."

Siberia Ida was sentenced to four years of exile in Siberia. She was sent to a frigid outpost called Krivosheino, where she was the only woman among 60 male criminals. She slept with an ax under her bed to protect herself. Living in a hut with no running water, she had to carry water, kindling wood, and other provisions long distances. When it got dark, she locked herself in and spent the long cold nights in complete isolation. Her only companion was a collie named Pizer. After Ida's release in 1982, the authorities continued their harassment. She was given 72 hours to leave her family's apartment in Moscow and refused a residence permit to live anywhere else. After six months of wandering, she was finally allowed to settle in Bendery, Moldavia, hundreds of miles from her friends in Moscow.

Ida was not allowed to travel, even to get treatment for her severe heart and kidney ailments, and was thrown off trains and buses. She coped with her isolation by devoting herself to working for other refuseniks, writing so many letters that she developed medical problems in her hands.

Ida Nudel welcomed by President Chaim Herzog at the President's Residence in Jerusalem, October 18, 1987.

"Guardian angel" During her entire period of refusal, Ida Nudel worked ceaselessly to help others in the same situation, especially those who were imprisoned in labor camps. She became known as the "guardian angel of the prisoners of conscience," a symbol of strength and hope for thousands.

"My guiding principle was to help those who did not have others helping them," she said. "I saw from my own experience how terrible it was to be left alone without anyone back home in support." She sent countless letters and packages, intervened with the authorities, and gave the prisoners' families practical and emotional support. She understood that for prisoners who felt that they were alone, contact with the outside was as important as food. She organized letter-writing campaigns and saw to it that prisoners got dozens of telegrams on their birthdays.

Ida Nudel meets her sister at the Tel Aviv airport, October 15, 1987.

At the same time others were working for her release. Jane Fonda visited her in April 1984. Los Angeles Mayor Tom Bradley, U.S. Congress Representative Pat Schroeder and actress Liv Ullmann all campaigned on her behalf. Eighty-nine members of the U.S. Congress signed a petition that was sent to Gorbachev in 1987. Then U.S. Secretary of State George Shultz, the late industrialist Armand Hammer, and Nobel Peace Prize winner Elie Wiesel—as well as thousands of ordinary citizens around the world—joined the campaign. It was Hammer who eventually brought Ida and her collie to Israel on his private jet.

After her arrival in Israel, Ida continued to fight for those who remained trapped in the Soviet Union and worked to facilitate the absorption of all new immigrants in Israel.

> "One's Jewishness means more than an awareness of Jewish history. It is an emotional and spiritual consciousness, an irrational feeling that I can't fully explain. It is also a sense of being linked with other Jews around the world. It is the knowledge that Jews all over the world would come to my defense if I needed them, and they have."
> — Ida Nudel

Maryam Mar'i

Maryam Mar'i was born in Acre in northern Israel in 1946, the youngest of 13 children of a traditional Moslem family. After graduating from a convent school in Acre, she studied education at the University of Haifa and went on to complete her master's and doctoral degrees at the University of Michigan, becoming one of a small handful of Israeli Arab women to hold a doctorate.

This achievement was not easy. Maryam's father was 74 when she was born. When she reached 10th grade, he announced that it would be her last year of school—there was no need for a girl to study any further. Maryam, who had already dreamed of university studies, realized that rebelling directly against her father would be futile. "I sensed that I must change his way of thinking, his viewing me as a woman whose only role is in the home," she says.

Communication Maryam invoked the support of her oldest brother. This was not easy. He was a refugee in Lebanon having fled Acre during the 1948 war and was not allowed to return. Writing to this brother, whom she had known only when she was a baby, she asked for his intervention. In a letter to their father, Maryam's brother explained that, in the politically volatile Middle East, a woman should have an education that would allow her to work if necessary. After reading the letter carefully, her father—then 90 years old—summoned the entire family. He announced that from then on the oldest of the brothers living with the family would be responsible for such matters as Maryam's education. He explained that the world had changed so much during his lifetime that he feared making wrong decisions that could cause suffering.

Maryam Mar'i

PROFILES OF WOMEN 95

Traditional Games

The Early Childhood Education Center (see page 97) has recently produced a video film on play, designed both to show teachers and parents the value of play and to document traditional games that are in danger of disappearing. Most of the traditional games are not competitive and serve as a force for socialization—bringing the individual into a group. "They're the antithesis of Western individualism," says Maryam. She hopes families will come to appreciate these traditional games, which all use natural or easily-made materials, rather than aspiring only to Barbie dolls, Lego, or electronic games which most families cannot afford.

One game uses an embroidered cloth as a "board" and seashells gathered at the beach as markers. Another game, similar to jacks, is played with leg joint bones saved from the lambs traditionally eaten on special occasions. Another, similar in principle to chess, is played outdoors. Holes are made in the earth or sand, and stones (or these days sometimes bottle caps) are used as "soldiers." It was discovered that only a few elderly men in one village still know this game, which, according to tradition, the Prophet Mohammed used to play in the sands of the Arabian desert.

Maryam sees this episode as vital in shaping her thinking. She feels that the way she gained her freedom to study—through communication rather than confrontation—helped her family learn to accept and appreciate her independence. This process, she believes, also taught her the importance of initiating change in her community at large while at the same time respecting traditional values. Maryam has written several important studies of Arab women's roles in a traditional society undergoing profound change—change that her own experience vividly illustrates.

Words in action Maryam's focus is not theory but action. Her interests are women, children and dialogue to solve the political conflict. For her, these areas are all connected. For true dialogue, she says, "we must have something to offer the other side. We must come from a position of pride and strength." She believes that the most effective way to strengthen Arab society is by working with children and women—mothers and teachers—who raise and educate them in their early years. "People said I was withdrawing by focusing on early childhood education rather than political action, but I don't see it that way," she says. Improving the education of Arab children—teaching them to think clearly and solve problems, strengthening their identity and appreciation of their own heritage—will lead to true change and thus has far-reaching political implications, she maintains.

An Arab nursery school.

The Early Childhood Education Center

Maryam devotes most of her energies to the Acre-based Early Childhood Education Center, which she helped initiate and now directs. Founded eight years ago by a group of Arab professional women, the center trains teachers and caregivers for day care centers, nursery schools, and kindergartens.

An important part of the program, says Maryam, is strengthening the confidence of the women trainees themselves, freeing them from their traditional conditioning to be passive and obedient. In order to resist long-standing ideas that early childhood programs should merely keep children clean and quiet, the women must become leaders and initiators themselves, she says.

The center also produces its own learning materials, designed to stimulate children and help strengthen their identity. Now in production is an education kit on Ramadan, the month of fasting observed by religious Moslems. Maryam believes there will be a market for such materials in other Arab countries as well.

Maryam Mar'i and Leah Shakdiel at a dialogue meeting.

Dialogue Maryam has participated in several groups devoted to Arab-Jewish dialogue and the search for peace and coexistence. She is currently active in the Women's Peace Network, an organization of Arab and Jewish women. "Cultural and religious differences are not what divide us," she says. "We can learn about each other and these differences enrich us. What divides us is the political conflict." Maryam supports the Palestinian struggle for independence and a Palestinian state as the solution to the conflict.

Maryam traces her faith in the value of dialogue to her teenage years, when she helped her family understand her desire to study and develop in her own way, even though her path diverged from tradition. It is this belief in the worth of true communication that has encouraged her to work for Arab-Jewish dialogue. The process has never been easy, she says. But despite many painful and discouraging experiences, her faith has been reinforced by honest exchanges that have transformed hostility into understanding.

Leah Shakdiel

In 1978 Leah Shakdiel, a 27-year-old teacher, joined a group of idealists who settled in Yeroham, a small development town in southern Israel. The group was madeup of young people committed to both the Jewish religious tradition and to values of peace, human rights, and equality. Hoping to contribute to Israeli society, she felt that the best thing she could do was to teach in an outlying place like Yeroham instead of choosing a more comfortable life in one of the major cities.

Most of the people of Yeroham, originating in Rumania, North Africa, India, and elsewhere, immigrated to Israel in the 1950s. The community faced many social, economic, and educational challenges; there was much to be done.

Teaching Leah began to teach Hebrew and Jewish studies to adults as well as children. "I was an involved teacher, with a community orientation," she says. "In a small place like Yeroham, teaching adults is a very significant means of social change."

In 1983 Leah was elected to the Yeroham town council. Getting involved in local politics grew naturally out of her motives for living in Yeroham—to improve the quality of life in the community. She hoped to promote the idea among the people—most of whom did not grow up within a democratic system—that democracy offers ways of making things happen, of working for goals, rather than relying on other powerful people or on luck.

She was the first woman elected to the Yeroham town council. Most of the residents held traditional Middle-Eastern views and were not used to women in politics. But Yeroham is very tolerant, says Leah. "It is a very warm place. Not everyone may have understood me fully but they were willing to live with me and work with me." In local politics in a place like Yeroham, says Leah, "everything is connected to everything else." Women's studies, the civil rights of the neighboring Bedouins, religious affairs, economic independence—all have to do with creating a better community. She has been active in all these areas.

A Jewish immigrant from Cochin, India. Indian Jews were among those who settled in Yeroham, the development town where Leah Shakdiel lives.

PROFILES OF WOMEN 99

Women's rights Leah Shakdiel became well-known as a women's rights activist in 1986. She was then nominated to serve on the Yeroham religious services council, a public body supervising and budgeting for the local religious facilities such as synagogues and cemeteries. No such council in Israel had ever included a woman.

Leah Shakdiel's nomination became an issue of national debate. When she was refused the seat, she petitioned the Supreme Court. She invoked Israel's Declaration of Independence, which provides for equality of social and political rights regardless of religion, race, or sex. In 1988 the Court handed down a landmark ruling upholding her right to serve on the council. Leah Shakdiel's struggle was important for many reasons.

First of all, she set a precedent that allowed women to serve on what had been an all-male body. She feels that this was particularly important for the religious community to which she belongs. In this community, she says, it has become quite acceptable for women to work in medicine, law and other professions, but some still look askance at women taking an active part in public life along with men. Citing rabbis who were staunch supporters of women's suffrage in the 1920s, when it was still new in the U.S., Leah would like to see her community honor the best of its tradition regarding the role of women.

Secondly and more broadly, Leah Shakdiel represents something very central—and very problematic—in a modern democratic society rooted in an ancient tradition. It is inevitable that modernity and tradition will conflict at certain points. Leah works within these areas of conflict and attempts to resolve them.

As an orthodox Jew, one who lives within the framework of the religious commandments, Leah is committed to both the religious tradition and to feminism. This combination is not always easy. Yet she believes that we can be faithful to the past while at the same time enhancing women's roles within the framework of the tradition. "We have to take every step and examine it and see if the time is right for it," she says.

There are, she believes, many steps that are now timely. Women can sit on administrative bodies—such as religious services councils—that do not make decisions regarding religious law. Women can study the Jewish law, something that has begun to happen on a large scale during the past decade. "It will change the nature of the Jewish community in a few generations once you have women who know the law," says Leah. Women's roles in the synagogue can also be enhanced within the bounds of religious law.

A just society For Leah Shakdiel, a mother of three, women's issues represent just one aspect of working toward a more just society, an ideal she is pursuing on many fronts. In addition to chairing the committee on women's status of Na'amat, Israel's largest women's organization, she is active in the religious peace group Oz V'Shalom and the Association for Civil Rights in Israel, and continues to serve on the Yeroham religious services council.

Her main efforts are devoted to what she calls "community building" in Yeroham. Leah Shakdiel now directs the town's culture center, conducting a variety of programs for groups ranging from preschool children to the elderly. A main focus is to cultivate a sense of achievement among the people of Yeroham—"many of whom feel they are less than what they should be—and foster their belief that there is no limit to what they can be."

A key part of this effort is to document the saga of immigration and development—the struggle of people who came to the country with very little, settled in an isolated place, and had to somehow feed their families. They not only survived but created a unique community, says Leah. Central to this documentation project is a local museum of the community's development. "It is a story of suffering and heroism, of disappointment and great achievement, and after 40 years it's time it was recognized and recorded," says Leah Shakdiel. "The development town is a unique form of community, like the kibbutz, and deserves a special place in Israel's history."

Leah Shakdiel sees Yeroham as a microcosm of Israeli society, and of the challenge of making that society what it should be. "Something new is being created here," she says. "We simply decide whether to take an active role in the process, or to live through it as best we can, accepting whatever happens to us." Leah Shakdiel has clearly chosen the former.

Leah with her children.

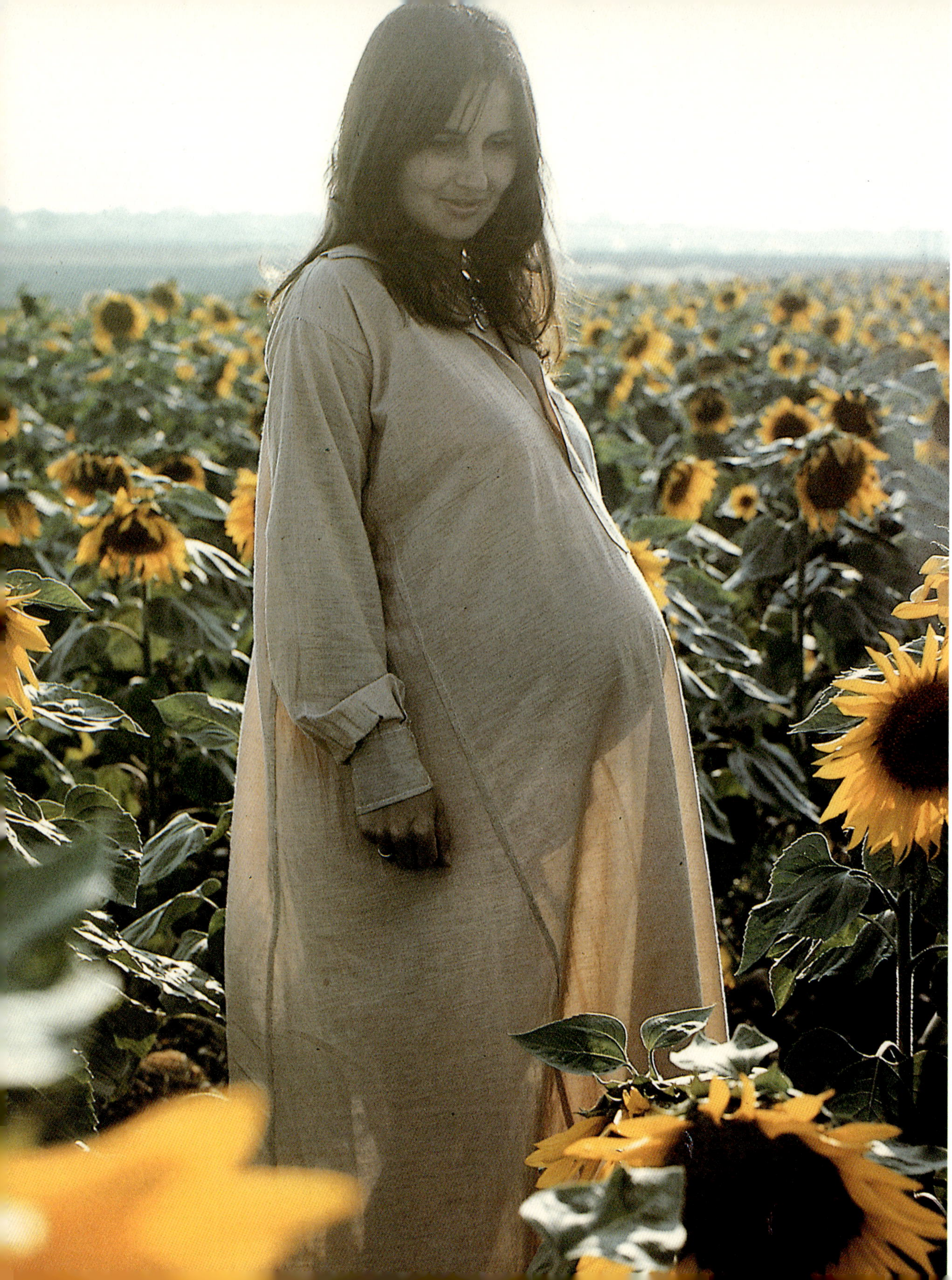

chapter six

A Lifetime

Family ties are important at every stage of life. In general, girls grow up in a warm context of parents, siblings, grandparents, aunts, uncles, and cousins. They see marriage and motherhood as central to their futures. Whenever possible, teenagers away from home in the army or at university go home for the Sabbath and holidays. Whether one is religious or not, holidays are times for the family to be together. Very few women postpone marriage or even motherhood in order to establish their careers; the tendency is rather to try to do it all at once. Older women devote much of their time to being grandmothers.

Arab society is in a state of flux; with many variations along the continuum between tradition and modernity at every stage of life. Yet family remains a powerful force. The expectation that a girl will grow up to be a wife and mother is even stronger than in the Jewish community.

Birth

In the Jewish community, the birth of a son or a daughter is cause for great joy. But while the religious tradition dictates the circumcision ceremony at the age of eight days for boy babies, there is no parallel traditional ceremony to mark the birth of girls. Sometimes a daughter is named and welcomed into the community at a special ceremony at the synagogue on a Sabbath soon after her birth. Some families have begun to create their own ceremonies to celebrate the birth of their daughters.

Opposite: Motherhood

Right: Wearing a headscarf is usual for the more religious.

A LIFETIME 103

A first school class.

These celebrations have become popular enough that they have a name. It is called *simhat bat*, rejoicing for a daughter. A *simhat bat* ceremony can feature biblical verses as well as selections from modern literature which express the parents' joy and thankfulness at bringing a new life into the world. Children are often named for grandparents or other relatives, who may be remembered in the ceremony.

School

Israeli elementary schools operate on a short day (eight in the morning until 12 or one), six days a week (Sunday through Friday for the Jewish schools). Classes average between 30 and 40 pupils. Compared to American schools, there is less formality. Pupils call their teachers and often even the principal by their first names.

Most elementary school children attend neighborhood schools but may go further away for high school. Jewish and Arab students attend schools belonging to separate systems.

The Jewish public school system is divided into state secular (the largest group) and state religious schools, as well as independent schools for the ultra-Orthodox. Many of the religious schools (and all of the ultra-Orthodox) have separate classes for boys and girls.

The Arab schools have their own curriculum, which is similar to that of the Jewish schools but includes the Islamic religious tradition and literature. The language of instruction is Arabic; English and Hebrew are taught as second languages. Boys and girls sit in the same class in most elementary and high schools. In towns where the Islamic movement is strong, many girls wear the traditional full-length gowns with head coverings. They may sit in the same classrooms as girls wearing jeans.

104 A LIFETIME

Fighting stereotypes

Studies have shown that textbooks fail to reflect the actual roles of men and women in society. One study showed that elementary school readers depicted men in 140 different occupations and women in only 13 (even when "mother," "sister," and "grandmother" were counted as occupations). As a result, the Education Ministry and other bodies have been developing curriculum materials that give children a less stereotyped and more accurate picture of men's and women's roles.

These new materials are designed to help free children from sexist stereotypes such as "boys don't cry" or "girls are fearful" and allow both boys and girls to be sometimes gentle and sometimes assertive, sometimes dependent and sometimes independent. One of these new books begins by talking about stereotypes and how they shape our thinking—for example, in films and TV programs the good, successful people are almost always good-looking—and then goes on to define sexism as stereotypes about males and females.

Exercises help students think about what has shaped their ideas of what boys and girls can do. One exercise has children write about themselves—what toys they were given, things they do with their fathers, things they do with their mothers, what their fathers/mothers do at home, their own jobs at home, people they would like to emulate, advice their parents and teachers give them about their future.

High school

While elementary school children attend their local neighborhood schools, students usually choose a high school, not necessarily in the neighborhood, among a variety of academic and vocational tracks. It is not unusual (especially in the religious school system) to attend a residential high school in a different city and come home only every week or two for the Sabbath.

Many high schools have more applicants than places and competition is stiff. At the age of 13 or 14, many students face a battery of aptitude tests, entrance exams, and interviews that is in some ways comparable to college application in the U.S.

Another major fact of life for Israeli high school students is the matriculation exams. These tests, in math, English, history, Bible, Hebrew language and literature, sciences, and other subjects, carry a lot of weight in determining one's chances for university entrance (also highly competitive), jobs, and almost anything else one might want to do in the future. Usually taken in the 11th and 12th grade, the matriculation exams are a source of much pressure for students.

Youth movements

For many girls (and boys), a youth movement is an important part of growing up. The youth movements in Israel are just that—run almost entirely by youth, with little interference from parents, teachers, or anyone else representing the adult establishment. High school students serve as group leaders for elementary school children. The director of a youth movement center is often a young person doing the job as part of his or her army service; usually no one over about 21 is on the scene.

Most youth movements meet every Tuesday and Saturday (Sabbath) afternoon. High schools dismiss their students early on Tuesdays to accommodate the youth movement schedules. Activities include discussions of current events in Israel and the world, games, sports, scouting, singing (loud!) and dancing. A popular activity for children of elementary school age is a "treasure hunt" that involves looking for clues hidden at various locations around the city. During school vacations, the youth movements organize hikes and camping trips.

There are over 10 active youth movements, many with specific religious or political affiliations. Among the largest is the Scouts, with separate Arab and Jewish groups. The Israeli Scouts (which are not separated into boy and girl scouts) are part of the World Boy and Girl Scouts' Associations. Many of the youth movements form groups that go to the army together. Their service may be work at a kibbutz, sometimes with the goal of establishing a new kibbutz, or community work in the cities.

Many high school students lead groups of elementary school children in the Scouts or other youth movements. This is a major responsibility. It means planning and conducting activities twice a week, dealing with finances, taking groups of lively 10-year-olds on hikes through the desert, caring for children who get sick in the middle of a camping trip. For security reasons, all hikes and trips must be coordinated with the army and police, and there must be an armed escort (often a graduate of the movement who has finished his army service). This is all good preparation for the army, where many young people will carry even more responsibility.

Immigrants from the former Soviet Union at a youth camp.

A LIFETIME 107

Coming of age

The Jewish tradition considers a girl an adult at age 12 as far as observing the religious commandments is concerned. (For a boy, the age is 13.) Some girls at 12 begin lighting Sabbath and holiday candles, one of the religious commandments specifically for women. This new status, as well as the ceremony marking it, are called bat mitzvah. Traditionally, a girl at bat mitzvah is considered responsible for her own actions—and at 12 many do question their parents and teachers and make their own decisions. Bat mitzvah celebrations come in many kinds, varying according to the family's observance or non-observance of the religious tradition. Some families celebrate with a ceremony in the synagogue; others simply have a party at home or elsewhere.

Synagogue ceremony The ceremonies themselves vary greatly, reflecting the changing roles of women in religious life. In egalitarian synagogues (rare in Israel), where women play the same roles as men, a girl's bat mitzvah ceremony is the same as a boy's bar mitzvah ceremony. The girl usually reads a portion from the Torah scroll and a portion from the Prophets, chanting according to the traditional melody. This is a job that requires a lot of practice and the girl usually begins studying her reading months in advance. Sometimes she also gives a short speech about what she reads from the Bible. Many parents recite the blessing of thanksgiving celebrating every new occasion: "Blessed are You, Lord our God, King of the Universe, who has given us life, sustained us, and brought us to this moment."

In some synagogues, a girl does all these things, but in an all-women's prayer group. In synagogues where women don't take part, the girl's grandfather, father, or brothers may take certain roles in the service and the girl may receive a gift from the congregation. Sometimes a girl gives a talk about her Torah reading at a party for family and friends, but not at the synagogue. In some schools, the sixth grade has a shared bat mitzvah celebration for all the girls in the class. The "performance" part of the bat mitzvah—chanting and speaking before all one's friends and relatives who have been invited for the occasion—is not always easy, especially for girls who are shy. But most do a good job and enjoy the feeling of accomplishment.

Bat mitzvah parties These parties range from simple to quite elaborate. The main thing is celebrating together with family and friends. Grandparents, aunts, uncles, or others close to the bat mitzvah girl may speak to her in front of all the guests, remembering what she was like as a little girl and wishing her all good things for the future. They may

A bat mitzvah ceremony. For some others, bat mitzvah takes the form of a simple party at home.

offer her blessings recalling great women in Jewish tradition—"May you be as courageous as Deborah and as wise as Bruria." There is always food and often singing and dancing, and everyone brings the bat mitzvah girl a gift. Sometimes she has a separate party for her friends. However a bat mitzvah is celebrated, it is often the one day in a girl's life when she alone is the center of attention, and most enjoy it.

Arab girls There is no coming of age ceremony for Arab girls. Traditionally, when Arab girls reached the age of seven they were watched much more closely and not allowed to play with boys. (But in agricultural villages where every pair of hands was needed, boys and girls worked together in the fields and do so today.)

Today, for the most part, girls and boys are not strictly separated and most schools are mixed. After age 12 or 13, girls are generally more restricted in what they are allowed to do. For example, it would not be acceptable for a boy and a girl to travel together outside the town. In families that adhere to Moslem tradition, girls do not wear pants after age 13, but often wear a skirt on top of pants for modesty. Among strictly religious families, girls wear the traditional floor-length gown with a head cowl.

A LIFETIME 109

Army service

For many young women, entering the army is the major rite of passage. The army means more than leaving home for the first time. It is also the first chance—after 18 years of nurture, education, care and concern from parents and teachers—to make a serious contribution to society. Many young women see their military service in exactly these terms. For those willing to work hard, the army offers many challenges. A young woman can finish her two years of compulsory service with both professional skills and experience in making difficult decisions, handling serious responsibility, and working with people whose backgrounds may be radically different from her own.

Sergeant Einat: Tank instructor Einat is part of a carefully selected team of men and women who train recruits in the Israel Defense Forces Armor Corps. According to the tank school commander, the women on the team are doing a fine job in a tough field that was once the exclusive province of men.

During their training, Einat and the other team members learned to use the M-16 assault rifle and the Uzi submachine gun, and to strip, assemble, and fire the tank's 7.62 mm. machine gun and the 30- and 50-caliber Brownings. The women were treated exactly the same as the male trainees.

The women were under pressure all the time during training. Everything had to be done at top speed. When the tank needed servicing, they were black with grease from head to foot. The women had to lift the same things as the men, no matter how much they weighed, even heavy tank shells and 50-caliber machine guns. "The toughest job was changing the tracks," says Einat. "The bolts were so enormous that we had to jump on the wrench to tighten them."

One of the challenges of armor training is learning to drive the tank over rough country, up and down steep slopes, in and out of desert wadis. Einat says it helps the trainees when they see a woman driving the tank. "They say to themselves, if she can do it, so can I."

Sergeant Limor: Radar watch commander Up and down the Israeli coast, soldiers scan radar screens 24 hours a day, on the lookout for terrorist infiltrations from the sea. Sergeant Limor is a watch commander at one of these naval radar stations. One of the prerequisites for the job is good English. Part of the job is communicating with the captains of merchant vessels approaching the coast and verifying their identities.

When an operator spots a suspicious object on her screen, she informs Limor immediately. If necessary, she calls one of the missile boats or patrol boats at sea and asks for a check. "The commanders of the naval vessels are all men and officers. I'm a woman and a sergeant. But they always treat my warnings seriously. They have never failed to respond, even if they thought the object was harmless. They always check it out."

Limor and her team were involved in spotting the terrorist boats that approached the Israeli coast in May 1990. "I am convinced that if we hadn't spotted them, there would have been a terrible massacre on the beach. It's too awful to think about."

Lieutenant Michal: Education officer
Michal began her army service as a soldier-teacher, teaching Hebrew to new immigrant recruits. New in the country and new in the army, many of the soldiers faced numerous problems. Michal spent many hours listening, supporting, and helping.

After officers' training, Michal became a company commander, in charge of 30 to 40 new immigrant soldiers and the seven or eight teachers working with them. "I had a lot of power and faced many dilemmas about how to use it properly," she says. The major challenge was learning to respond to the soldiers' problems while maintaining her authority as an officer—not easy for a 19-year-old woman in command of men in their 20s. "During the first course, my impulse was to say yes to all their requests. After I saw that I had gone too far in that direction, in the second course my answer was always no. It was during the third course that I began to find the right approach."

Another major part of Michal's job as company commander was to supervise the teachers, who were a year younger than she was. Having finished her army service, Michal is now teaching high school and studying contemporary Jewish history at the university. Utilizing her military experience, she also directs army training courses for Hebrew teachers.

Members of the Israel Defense Forces.

A LIFETIME 111

Soldiers in training. After basic training, a wide range of responsible jobs are open to women in the army.

Responsibility Limor, Einat, and Michal do only a few of the numerous jobs open to women in the army. Others conduct psychological testing, serve as social workers in army jails, care for groups of Ethiopian children in residential schools, lead youth groups in disadvantaged neighborhoods, work as nature guides in field schools, maintain the optical instruments used by combat pilots. Some do such highly classified intelligence work that their parents are not allowed to know where they are stationed. The key word in all these jobs is responsibility—serious responsibility for other people's welfare, safety, and often their lives. For the young women willing to accept this responsibility, the army is a very real passage. If they enlist at 18 at the tail end of childhood, when they leave at 20 they are undoubtedly adults.

112   A LIFETIME

Dating

Israeli teenagers tend to do a lot in groups—movies, parties, hikes, trips. Many form strong friendships in high school that last a lifetime. Especially in religious circles, dating is less casual than in the U.S. It is more unusual for a girl to go out with one boy one week and another boy the next week. A couple's going out together tends to mean a more serious commitment, or at least an interest in one. It is not unusual for couples to form a serious relationship at age 15 or 16 and eventually marry often after army service).

Marriage

For the vast majority of both Jewish and Arab women, marriage is almost as natural as breathing. Marriage is widely seen not as a possible option, to be weighed against the advantages of independent singlehood, but as an important step in the normal course of life. Most Jewish women marry fairly soon after their army service; 80% of Israeli women are married by age 29 and 98% by age 40. Marriages are relatively stable; the Israeli divorce rate has consistently been 20 to 25% of the American rate.

In many ways, it is not easy to be a single woman in Israel. On both the public and private level, life revolves around the family. It is assumed that no one remains unmarried by choice, and a single woman's friends and relatives will make every effort to find her a suitable mate. Marriage bureaus and matrimonial ads in the newspapers abound. A single woman's friends will spend a lot of time talking about their children. Sabbath and holiday celebrations focus on traditional family meals, and many families invite single friends and relatives to join them on these days. At work, mothers receive paid leave if their children are ill, but a single woman has no equivalent privilege. For many years, singles did not receive the same housing loans as married couples.

A Jewish wedding ceremony.

Median age for first marriage:		
	Women	Men
Jews	22.8	25.9
Moslems	20	23.9
Christians	22.4	27.4
Druze	18.8	23.4

Marriages ending in Divorce:
Jewish: 1 out of 6
Druze: 1 out of 10
Moslem: 1 out of 11
Christian: very rare

The wedding ceremony

Jewish weddings are large joyful affairs, often attended by hundreds of guests. Dozens of rituals have grown up around the wedding ceremony. Some are religious obligations; others are custom. Some, like the henna ceremony, belong to specific ethnic groups; others are shared by almost all Jews. All these customs express the sanctity and seriousness as well as the joy of marriage.

There is no civil marriage in Israel; the ceremony is always religious. But beyond the ceremony itself, the families' attitudes toward the religious tradition have a lot to do with how they celebrate the wedding. Among many religious families, for example, men and women don't dance together but in separate circles.

Weddings are often celebrated on Tuesdays, the third day of the week. This is symbolically an auspicious day because it coincides with the third day of Creation, the day when the phrase "and God saw that it was good" appears twice in the biblical account.

A wedding celebration that follows religious custom may go something like this: According to religious law, the bride immerses in the *mikveh* (ritual bath) the night before the wedding (and every month thereafter). The bride and groom fast on the day of their wedding in recognition of the seriousness of the responsibility they are undertaking. According to tradition, fasting symbolizes atonement for past sins, which are all forgiven as the couple begins their new life together.

Before the ceremony, the bride sits on a special chair decorated with flowers. Her mother, mother-in-law, other women in the family and close friends stay with her while the guests come up to congratulate her.

The groom, led by his male friends and relatives with singing and dancing, goes to the bride and lifts the veil over her face. He recites the biblical verse "O sister! May you become [the mother of] thousands of myriads" (Genesis 24:60).

The ceremony itself is held under a special canopy, a prayer shawl or specially decorated cloth supported by four poles, called a *huppa*. Friends or relatives hold each of the poles.

The two fathers escort the groom to the wedding canopy, and the two mothers, often holding candles, escort the bride. Traditionally, the bride and groom are like a queen and king on their wedding day, and are always accompanied by an entourage. Under the canopy, the bride circles the groom seven times and the ceremony begins.

In the central act of the ceremony, the groom places the ring on the bride's right index finger and recites the traditional formula: "Behold you are consecrated to me with this ring according to the Law of Moses and Israel." Performed before two witnesses, this act legalizes the marriage.

The marriage contract is read and given to the bride. Then close friends, relatives or other honored guests are called to the wedding canopy to chant each of the seven traditional wedding blessings. These blessings praise the Creator of all life, the Source of the joy of the bride and groom. After the bride and groom drink from the same cup of wine, the groom breaks a glass with his foot. The breaking of something whole symbolizes imperfection—the suffering and sorrow in the world that are remembered even at a moment of great personal joy. The religious ceremony ends when the couple retire to a private room to break their fast together, symbolizing the beginning of their lives together as husband and wife.

The henna ceremony is a pre-wedding ceremony, not held at the wedding itself.

> It was an ancient custom to plant a cedar tree when a boy was born and a pine tree when a girl was born. When the children grew up and married, the trees were used for posts for their wedding canopies.

Wedding according to Islamic law For Moslems, the marriage becomes legal when the groom presents the bride with a possession of his—now usually a ring— and recites the traditional formula before two witnesses. Then the marriage contract is signed.

The contract states how much the groom "pays" for the bride—now a purely symbolic transaction—and how the couple's property will be divided in the event of divorce. The Islamic wedding ceremony sometimes takes place at the time of engagement, which could be a year before the wedding. After the ceremony is performed, the couple can spend time together—go to a movie, go shopping, prepare their home—with the approval of the community, but they do not live together or consummate the marriage. Although the ceremony makes the contract legal according to Islamic law, the marriage is not accepted by the community until it is celebrated publicly. Celebrations vary. Families in cities may rent a hall and the bride often wears a Western-style white dress. Rural families may invite the whole village to a traditional seven-day celebration. Despite the popularity of Western-style celebrations, a growing sense that important customs are in danger of disappearing is leading more families to choose traditional seven-day feasts.

Home and family

Israel is one of the most "pro-natal" societies in the world—that is, having children, in some circles the more the better, is viewed as highly desirable. The

The Henna Ceremony

Many brides of North African and Middle Eastern origin (or those who marry men in these groups) celebrate the henna ceremony before their weddings. While most get married in a Western-style white dress, they wear traditional garb for the henna. For the Yemenite bride, this is a special dress of brocade or embroidered fabric, a heavy headdress encrusted with beads and ornaments and often topped with flowers, and dozens of ornate filigree necklaces, bracelets, and rings, all with symbolic significance.

A reddish paste made from the powdered roots or leaves of the henna plant is rubbed on the hands of the bride and the guests. Once seen as a good omen and symbol of fertility, the henna ceremony is now held more as a link with one's heritage before the wedding itself is celebrated in more or less Western style.

Traditionally an occasion for women only, the henna celebration may now include many of the male and female wedding guests. What used to be a week-long ritual in Yemen, for example, has been shortened to one evening.

Yet parts of the tradition are preserved. In the Yemenite community, older women act as "dressers," helping brides outfit themselves properly in the elaborate costume and ornaments that belong to the community and are lent to each bride in turn. Women singers and drummers serenade the bride with traditional melodies.

idea of zero population growth has no following in Israel. More than a personal decision, having children is viewed as affecting the welfare of the country as a whole.

In the early years of the state, Prime Minister David Ben Gurion established prizes for families with 10 or more children. He once said, "Any Jewish woman who, as far as it depends on her, does not bring into the world at least four healthy children is shirking her duty to the nation, like a soldier who evades military service. And it is the duty of the Jewish people as a whole to provide women with the economic, cultural, and social conditions to enable them to give these children a proper upbringing and education."

Among religious Jews, the biblical commandment to "be fruitful and multiply" is taken quite seriously. In addition, certain historical and demographic factors are important:

The World War II Holocaust, in which six million Jews were killed and an entire culture was wiped out, was a trauma whose proportions can barely be grasped. Its effects are felt in Israel in many ways. One is the sense that, although no human being who is lost can be replaced, the Jews are obligated to try to remedy this demographic disaster.

Israel is a small country surrounded by large countries with which it is unfortunately not at peace. The population of the surrounding Arab countries is well over a dozen times that of Israel and is growing far more rapidly. Tragically, Israel has been involved in six wars in 43 years and has never known peace. Many thousands of young lives have been lost. Most families do not necessarily talk or even think about history and demography when deciding when to have children, or how many children—they simply want children, love children, and cannot imagine their lives without children. Yet while it may remain largely unspoken, there is a life-affirming impulse: a wish to create life in the face of too much death.

Babies in the baby house in a kibbutz.

A LIFETIME 117

Pro-children policies

Certain public policies encourage and support large families.

The National Insurance Institute (roughly parallel to the American Social Security Administration) allots families monthly payments according to the number of children in the family, regardless of income. All women receive a special allowance with the birth of each child. Families with four or more children receive discounts for public child care and summer camps; larger families receive tax discounts.

A well-developed mother and child health care system provides free care for pregnant women and vaccinations and routine checkups for babies.

Day care, subsidized mostly by the Labor Ministry and operated by various women's organizations, is widely available (although the demand still exceeds the supply). A baby can be registered at six months and continue in day care until first grade. The centers are open from 7:30 a.m.. until 4:00 p.m.

Legislation for working mothers allows paid maternity leave and time off to care for children who are ill (see chapter 2). Working mothers are entitled to take off six days a year to tend to their children's needs.

Fertility technology is well-developed. Israeli doctors are leaders in the field and state-of-the-art techniques are available. The average number of children in a family is as follows: Moslems 4.6; Druze 4.2; Christians 2.6; Jews 2.8

Sharing roles

Despite a definite trend toward the sharing of responsibility, especially among younger families, it is still usually the woman who carries most of the responsibility for home and family. Many husbands help by picking up the children at kindergarten, buying groceries, hanging out the laundry, washing the dishes and doing many other jobs. It isn't unusual to see a man in uniform with his rifle slung over his shoulder, wheeling his child in a stroller to the day care center on his way to reserve army duty.

Yet it is often the wife who delegates these tasks and bears ultimate

Children are looked after communally in a kibbutz.

A father looks after the children.

responsibility for making sure they get done. And many men still expect to find a clean house and a meal on the table when they come home, even though their wives may be working as many hours as they are.

A few years ago, the *Na'amat* women's organization ran a campaign designed to encourage men to do more around the house. The slogan, promoted on posters, radio, and TV, was: "Be a man, give her a hand." Some women felt the approach was wrong, that the emphasis should be on *sharing*, rather than *helping*, but Na'amat felt it best to begin with an appeal that was closer to the way most families actually operate.

And while many working mothers often feel overextended and frazzled at the edges, they like taking care of their home and family, see it as a major source of gratification, and don't necessarily want to give it up (although few would object to sharing!). Due to their investment in family responsibilities and the short school day, many women work part time. (Among Jewish women, 64% of mothers of children under 15 work, but 42% of all working women work part-time.)

Passover

Some traditional women of Middle Eastern origin start preparing for Passover as early as December. They begin by cleaning the rice that will be eaten on the holiday, checking to make sure no forbidden materials were mixed in it during harvesting or storage. Anthropologist Susan Starr Sered, who has studied the religious lives of traditional Middle Eastern women, describes the process: The women sort through the rice grain by grain, going through it seven times in order to clean it properly. Many of these women cook for large extended families and so sort through 10 or 15 kilograms of rice in this painstaking manner.

The elaborate rice-cleaning, says Sered, is actually a religious act. Sered sees this as just one of many rituals developed by the elderly women she observed. Without formal education, they are excluded from the male-dominated realms of prayer and study but have developed their own religious lives, centered on home and family.

She noted that the women seemed to prefer preparing food in elaborate and time-consuming ways—for example, stuffed grape leaves and other vegetables that are delicious but take hours to prepare. "Cooking for holidays turns the profane act of cooking into a sacred ritual," she says. "These women opt to do this work because for them, it is a type of divine worship. They do it to please God." (Susan Starr Sered, *Women as Ritual Experts*)

The calendar

In a country with three Sabbaths—Friday for the Moslems, Saturday for the Jews, and Sunday for the Christians—things can be somewhat complicated. In predominantly Moslem Arab towns, elementary schools are closed on Friday and Saturday, high schools on Friday only. But if the town is mixed Moslem and Christian, schools and workplaces may be closed on Friday and Sunday but opened on Saturday. On the other hand, in towns where the population is mainly Christian and many work in the Jewish sector, schools and workplaces may be closed on Saturday and Sunday.

The Jewish calendar

For both religious and non-religious Jews, the rhythm of life is determined by the Jewish calendar. Saturday is the Sabbath, observed by some in synagogue and traditional family meals and by some at the beach—but for the entire Jewish population it is a much-anticipated day off from work. For those who observe the Sabbath, much of Friday is spent in preparation for it—shopping, cooking, and cleaning. Friday is the traditional day for these tasks regardless of religious observance. All holidays involve special preparations and special foods, none more than Passover—the spring holiday commemorating the Exodus of the Jews

A volunteer helps out with the elderly.

from Egypt. The religious laws for Passover prohibit eating leavened foods—most baked goods and grains—or keeping any in one's possession. Different dishes or those that have been cleaned by special processes are used. Going far beyond the requirements of religious law, many women, whether they are strictly observant or not, prepare for Passover with elaborate and exhausting spring cleaning rites. Beds are put out on sidewalks, the contents of closets on porches. Anything movable is moved. Every object in the house is dismembered and scrubbed. The entire house is often painted.

Grandmothers

Ties between the generations are usually strong. For many older women, being a grandmother is a central occupation. Busy working mothers often rely on the grandmothers to help care for their children. At the same time, daughters are often involved in the care of an elderly parent who needs assistance. (Only about 5% of the aged in Israel live in old age homes or other institutions.) Thus a woman at midlife may find herself not only working and raising her own younger children, but also helping care for a married daughter's children and tending to the needs of an

A LIFETIME

Yemenite grandmothers weave colorful baskets for the traditional henna ceremony.

elderly parent at the same time. These family obligations make for busy days, but they are usually seen as natural and important parts of adult life. The later years—after retiring from work and after the children are grown—are also a time of freedom for many women, a chance to pursue activities there was never time for while working and raising a family. Popular among these activities are volunteering and study.

Volunteering There is a long Jewish tradition of helping the needy in the community, and much of this work was always done by women. It is thus not surprising that many women turn to volunteer activities of some sort when they finally have some free time. Some simply involve themselves in visiting the sick, tutoring disadvantaged children, or helping new immigrants through informal networks of family, neighbors, and friends. Others join programs organized by such groups as the Na'amat women's organization. Through Na'amat, tens of thousands of women do volunteer work ranging from taking disabled persons to health clinics to sorting uniforms for the army.

Neighborhoods in many cities have organized networks in which retired people tend to less able elderly persons in the community. In one Tel Aviv neighborhood, retired residents have compiled a list of every elderly person living alone. The volunteers call everyone at regular intervals and help with cooking, shopping, or just going out for a walk if necessary. Says one of the volunteers: "Just as I have to remember if I owe money at the grocery store, I have to remember that I owe something to society, to others who need help."

One woman who had been in the Russian cavalry in her youth volunteers at a rehabilitative horseback riding program for children with developmental problems.

In another program, a group of elderly women run a laundry service for the disabled in their community together with a group of high school students. The women sort, iron, and fold; the teenagers pick up and deliver.

Learning Many women see the third age (following the "first age" of youth and the "second age" of work and family) as a chance to study—to learn a new field that has always intrigued them or pick up studies that had to be dropped when they were occupied full time with job and children. Courses run by the Education Ministry, universities, community centers, synagogues and private institutes abound. Many thousands of retirees throughout the country are studying everything from video film production to Bible to art history.

The Tehila Program

Established in 1977, Tehila (Hebrew for "praise") is a basic education and literacy program designed to meet the needs of special groups. Some are Arab women who grew up before Israel's compulsory education law was enacted. Many are Jewish women who immigrated to Israel in the 1950s from Middle Eastern countries where girls did not attend school. The following decades of their lives were spent in hard work, many raising large families under difficult conditions. It was only after their children were grown that they had a chance to begin the education that circumstances never allowed them.

During the course of the Tehila program, women who didn't know the alphabet begin writing letters to their children and grandchildren in the army and studying the Bible.

Manana, a mother of 10 who works as a cleaning woman in a northern development town, was asked by her friends why she wanted to begin learning at her age. "Suppose I were going up four flights of stairs," she responded, "and I didn't find the light switch until the third flight. Should I continue walking in the dark, or turn on the switch and enjoy the light until the end?"

Women Firsts

Sirimavo Bandaranaike	(b. 1916) She became the first woman prime minister in the world when her party, the Sri Lanka Freedom Party, won the general election in July 1960. Her husband was prime minister of Sri Lanka when he was assassinated in 1959. She led her husband's party to victory in the 1960 elections.
Sarah Breedlove	(1867–1919) Also known as Madame C.J. Walker, she was the first self-made millionairess. An uneducated African-American orphan from Louisiana, U.S.A., she founded her fortune on a hair straightener.
Nadia Comaneci	(b. 1961) The Rumanian girl was the first gymnast ever to achieve a perfect score (10.00) in the Olympic Games in Montreal in 1976. In all, she had 7 perfect scores at the Games.
Marie Curie	(1867–1934) A Polish-born French physicist, she is famous for her work on radioactivity. She was the first woman to win the Nobel Prize for Physics in 1903, together with Antoine Henri Becquerel. She was also the first woman to win the Nobel Prize for Chemistry in 1911.
Katherine Dunham	(b. 1910) American dancer, choreographer and anthropologist who was the first person to organize a black dance troupe of concert calibre, in 1940. A popular entertainer who toured the United States and Europe, she was also a serious artist intent on tracing the roots of black culture.
Amelia Earhart	(1897–?) She was one of the world's most celebrated aviators and the first woman to fly alone over the Atlantic Ocean on May 20–21, 1932. In 1935, she made a solo flight from California to Hawaii, the first person to fly this route successfully. In 1937, she set out to fly around the world with a navigator. Two-thirds through the distance, her plane disappeared in the central Pacific.
Gertrude Ederle	(b. 1906) One of the best known American sports persons of the 1920s, she was the first woman to swim the English Channel, on August 6, 1926. She swam the 35 miles from Cap Gris-Nez, France, to Dover, England, in 14 hours 31 minutes, breaking the existing men's record by 1 hour 59 minutes.
Dame Naomi James	The New Zealander is the first woman to sail round the world solo, in the cutter *Express Crusader*. She sailed from Dartmouth, England, on September 9, 1977 and reached the same port on June 8, 1978. It took her 265 sailing days to complete the journey.
Selma Lagerlöf	(1858–1940) The first woman and also the first Swedish writer to win the Nobel Prize for Literature in 1909. A novelist whose work is rooted in legend

	and saga, she is said to rank among the most naturally gifted of modern storytellers.
Lucretia Mott and Elizabeth Cady Stanton	They founded the organized women's rights movment in the United States. In 1948 they organized the first Women's Rights Convention in the United States. Mott (1793–1880) also actively campaigned against slavery, and worked for voting rights and educational opportunities for freedmen after the Civil War. Stanton (1815–1902) went on to work with Susan B. Anthony for woman suffrage.
Florence Nightingale	(1820–1910) An English nurse, she was the founder of trained nursing as a profession for women. Because of the comfort and care she gave to wounded soldiers of the Crimean War (1854–) during the night rounds, she was dubbed "The Lady with the Lamp." In 1860 she established the Nightingale School for Nurses, the first of its kind in the world.
Margaret Sanger	(1883–1966) She is the founder of the birth control movement in the United States and international leader in the field. In 1916 she opened the first birth control clinic in the United States. In 1927 she organized the first World Population Conference in Geneva, Switzerland. She was the first president of the International Planned Parenthood Federation.
Junko Tabei	(b. 1939) A Japanese housewife, she was the first woman to reach the summit of Mt. Everest on May 16, 1975. She was part of the first all-woman (and all-Japanese) team to reach the summit.
Valentina V. Tereshkova	(b. 1937) A Russian cosmonaut, she was the first woman to travel in space from June 16 to 19, 1963. She was in space for 70 hours and 50 minutes. She volunteered for the cosmonaut program in 1961, and was accepted on the basis that she was an accomplished amateur parachutist, although she had no pilot training.
Baroness Bertha von Suttner	(1843–1914) An Austrian novelist and pacifist, she was the first woman to win the Nobel Prize for Peace in 1905. In 1841 she founded an Austrian pacifist organization, and from 1892 to 1899 she edited the international pacifist journal *Die Waffen nieder!* (*Lay Down Your Arms!*).
Mary Wollstonecraft	(1759–1797) An English writer and advocate of educational and social equality for women, she was the author of *A Vindication of the Rights of Women* in 1792, the first major piece of feminist writing. The book, on a woman's place in society, pleads for the illumination of woman's mind.

Glossary

aliya	Literally, ascent; immigration to Israel; one of the waves of immigration.
bat mitzva	Ceremony marking the initiation of a girl at age 12 in to the Jewish religious community.
Conservative	Trend in Judaism which opposes extreme change in traditional observances while allowing certain modifications.
Eretz Israel	The land of Israel; Palestine.
Hagana	Jewish defense organization in pre-State Palestine.
Holocaust	The organized mass persecution and annihilation of the European Jews by the Nazis (1933–1945).
Hadith	The sayings and teachings of Muhammad that form a central part of Islamic dogma.
huppa	Wedding canopy.
intifada	The Palestinian uprising in the West Bank and Gaza Strip.
kibbutz	Communal settlement.
Knesset	Parliament of the State of Israel.
Koran	Sacred book of Islam, according to Islamic belief revealed by God to the prophet Muhammad.
Mishna	The earliest written collection of Jewish law after the Bible.
Orthodox	Strictly traditional trend in Judaism.
Palestine	Region in the eastern shore of the Mediterranean Sea that was the ancient Holy Land, sacred to Moslems, Christians and Jews. Parts of ancient Palestine are now in modern Israel and parts are in Jordan.
rabbanit	Learned woman; rabbi's wife.
Reform	Trend in Judaism which favors adapting tradition to conform with contemporary life and thought.
Reform	Trend in Judaism which favors adapting tradition to conform with contemporary life and thought.
Talmud	The compendium of Jewish religious law and tradition.
Torah	The biblical Five Books of Moses; the scroll containing these writings; the entire body of Jewish tradition and literature.
Yom Kippur	Day of Atonement, solemn fast day observed on the 10th day of the Jewish new year.
Zionism	Movement for a Jewish state in Palestine; support of the State of Israel.

Further Reading

Amiry, Suad and Tamari, Vera: *The Palestinian Village Home*, British Museum Publications Ltd, London, 1989.
Collins, Larry and Lapierre, Dominique: *O Jerusalem*, Grafton Books, London, 1982.
Elon, Amos: *A Day in the Life of the Israelis*, Thames and Hudson Ltd, London, 1985.
Gruber, Ruth: *Rescue: The Exodus of the Ethiopian Jews*, Atheneum, 1987.
Hannah Senesh: Her Life and Diary, Schocken Books, New York, 1972.
Meir, Golda: *My Life*, Dell Publishing Co., New York, 1975.
Minai, Naila: *Women in Islam*, Seaview Books, New York, 1981.
Shteiner, Puah: *Forever My Jerusalem*, Feldheim Publishers, Jerusalem/New York, 1987.
Shazar, Rachel Katznelson: *The Plough Woman: Memoirs of the Pioneer Women of Palestine* (first published in 1932), Herzl Press, New York, 1975.
Stowe, Harriet Beecher: *Woman in Sacred History: A Celebration of Women in the Bible* (first published in 1873), Portland House, New York, 1990.

Picture Credits

Anat Rotem-Braun 25, 31, 32, 36, 57, 60, 67, 77, 102, 103, 117.
Werner Braun 5, 10, 16, 23, 27, 30, 35, 37, 40, 42, 44, 45, 48, 49, 62, 71, 75, 78, 85, 88, 97, 99, 104, 109, 111, 112, 115, 118, 121.
Debbi Cooper 28, 29, 63, 73, 76, 101, 113, 119, 122.
Embassy of Israel, Singapore 33, 43 (poster), 56, 105.
Isaac Harari 46, 95, 98.
Israel Government Press Office 51, 53, 54, 55, 79, 91, 93, 94.
Jewish National Fund Photo Archives 19, 21, 26, 80, 107.
Life File/ Mike Evans 58, 65, 69.
The Jerusalem Report/ Elliot Hool 9.
Transglobe Agency 59.
Zionist Archives 81, 84.

The author wishes to thank Lisa Cooper, Alice Shalvi and Deborah Weissman for their valuable assistance.

Index

apostles 15
army service 38, 53, 76, 110–112
attitudes 7, 9, 11, 14, 21

babies 22, 34, 35
bat mitzvah 108–109
Bible 14
Birth 103, 104
bride 17, 63, 114–116
Bruria 7–9, 14
building 22–23

children 19, 22, 62, 117, 118
coming of age 108–109
community 9, 12, 18, 22, 27, 30, 73, 103

Damari, Shoshana 89–91
dating 113
daughter 7, 16, 17, 26, 62, 76
defense 24, 25
discrimination 31–32
divorce 14, 18, 30, 70
doctors 44, 45, 50

education 18, 19, 26, 37–39, 64, 73
equality 31–32, 64

family 9, 14, 22, 29, 34–35, 37, 59, 73, 116–117
father 8, 19, 33

girls 16, 37, 38, 39, 62, 103
grandmothers 86, 103, 121

Hebrew 19, 37, 41–43, 47, 56, 62
home 9, 11, 12, 14, 29, 116, 117
husband 8, 11, 14, 19, 62

immigrants (immigration) 18, 19, 23, 26, 28, 37, 40–42, 59–63
inheritance 14, 17
Israel Defense Forces 49, 77, 78, 110

Jews
 Ethiopian 62–63
 Yemenite 12, 60–61, 89

judges 13, 16, 18, 46, 47

kibbutz 22, 23, 33, 34, 35, 56, 86, 107
Knesset 25, 26, 28, 31, 47, 48

labor force 28, 30, 37
law(s) 9, 14, 17, 26, 30, 31, 46–47, 64, 70
lawyer 46, 50
leaders 12, 16, 30, 83
learning 123
literature 56–57

Mar'i, Maryam 95–98
marriage 14, 16, 18, 21, 22, 26, 30, 69, 70, 103, 113
maternity leave 32, 34
medicine 44–45, 64
Meir, Golda 48, 85–88
Mishna 14
missionaries 15
modesty 67
mother 9, 11, 13, 19, 21, 22, 32, 33, 34, 35, 44, 62, 70, 73, 103
mother-in-law 17, 47

neighbors 41, 61, 68, 76
nuns 74, 75
Nudel, Ida 92–94

Passover 120
pioneers 11, 18, 22, 33, 86
politics 28, 48–50
polygamy 18, 70
prayer 63, 64, 68
prophets 13, 15

rabbis, women 9, 66
rights 14
 equal 9, 24
 human 29
 legal 11
 property 26
 women's 29, 100
ruler 11

Sabbath 8, 14, 103, 106, 120

scholar 7, 11, 12, 13, 14
schools 26, 38, 39, 73, 74, 104–106
Senesh, Hannah 81–84
Shakdiel, Leah 99–101
simhat bat 104
social work 40
songs 12, 13, 16, 89, 90
sports 53–55
stereotypes 38, 105
study 63, 64, 68

Talmud 7, 8, 14, 39
teachers 11, 27, 42, 74, 85
teenager 16, 103
theater 50–52
tradition 7, 8, 9, 14, 16, 27, 59, 60, 62, 63—75, 103
transitions 63–75

universities 30, 47, 71, 92

volunteers 42, 83, 122
vote 18, 24, 25, 28, 70

war 59, 76–79
 World War I 21, 23, 86
 World War II 22, 34, 82
 Six Day War 30
 Yom Kippur War 76, 88
warrior 13, 16
weddings 12, 67, 114–116
wife (wives) 7, 9, 16, 17, 18, 21, 62, 70, 76, 103
women
 Arab 24, 27, 50, 69–73
 Christian 17, 74–75
 Druze 73, 74
 farmers 19, 21
 Jewish 19, 24
 Moslem 16, 17, 26
 ultra-Orthodox 66–68
Women of the Wall 65
Women in Black 76
Women in White 76
work 9, 20, 21, 23, 25, 28, 33–34, 59
workers 21, 23, 28

youth movements 106–107